EGREGIOUS ACTS: A MEMOIR OF VICTORY OVER VIOLENCE

LAKEACHA M. JETT

Most of the names in the text have been changed.

Copyright © 2012 by LaKeacha M. Jett.

All rights reserved, including the right of reproduction in whole or in part in any form.

Published by Jett Media Group, LLC

ISBN-13: 978-1477613801

ISBN-10: 1477613803

Printed in the United States of America

Cover designed by G.B. Designs

Cover photography by Lynette Jackson Photography

First paperback edition.

DEDICATION

This book is dedicated to my beautiful
daughter
Kaylah Alexiz Jett
You are who you are for a reason.
You're part of an intricate plan.
You're a precious, perfect and unique design
Called God's special little girl.
You look like you look for a reason.
Our God made no mistake.
He knit you together within the womb;
You're just what he wanted to make.
The parents you have were the ones he chose,
And no matter how you may feel,
They were custom-designed
with God's plan in mind,
And they bear the Master's seal.
No, that trauma you faced was not easy,
And God wept that it hurt you so;
But it was allowed to shape your heart,
So that into his likeness you'd grow.
You are who you are for a reason;
You've been formed by the Master's rod.
You are who you are, beloved, because there is
a God!
By Russell Kelfer
Love,
Mommy

INTRODUCTION

Infidelity and betrayal, lies and deceit, vengeance and violence. Those are only a few of the egregious acts that I encountered as I steadfastly held on to my desire to make something out of my life. I was determined that I would find real success. Never in a million years did I expect to face the difficulties that were awaiting me. A retrospective look at it all makes me wonder how I made it through without losing my mind.

One of the best ways to empower others is to share a portion of your experiences with them. This is exactly what I have done in *Egregious Acts: A Memoir of Victory Over Violence*. I've openly shared the intimate details of how a woman did all she could to destroy my life. I was burned alive while pregnant. The particulars of what happened before and after that are enough to make anyone throw in the towel. Yet, I persevered. I survived, and I'm here to share my story.

It is my greatest desire that this chronicle will encourage as many as possible to rise up out of any situation that has been holding you down. The things I endured could have easily had a permanently detrimental effect on my self-esteem, my mind and my desire to move forward with my life. I am convinced that my survival was not meant to be in vain.

Friend, you really can experience victory over violence. I look forward to hearing testimonies of other victories, and I pray that this book will have played a major role.

Agape,
Lady LaKeacha M. Jett

EGREGIOUS

Conspicuously and outrageously
bad
A crying shame
An egregious lie
A flagrant violation of human
rights
Gross injustice
Shocking

PROLOGUE

"Mommy, why are those scars on your neck?" As my daughter sits waiting for an answer, my mind retreats to November 16, 2000.

I'm screaming. "HELP ME! SOMEBODY CALL MARCUS! It's burning so badly! My skin is peeling off! My head is burning! I'm on fire! HELP ME!" The chemicals were burning my flesh quickly.

"Ma'am, calm down, calm down. We need to get these clothes off of you. Calm down, we will get Marcus."

The paramedic turned to a neighbor, "Who is this lady? Go in the house and get her purse." A few minutes later, "Ms. Jones, LaKeacha Jones. What happened to you? Who did this to you? Who is Marcus?" As the ambulance worker tried to gather information about me, I began to lose consciousness. I could hear, but no words exited my mouth. My thoughts had taken over.

I can't believe that Bitch attacked me. Ain't this some punk ass shit? It took three mutha' fuckers to sneak attack an eight months pregnant woman. This bitch has crossed the line. She got me this time. I'm going to kill that bitch. No BODY. No MURDER.

"Let's go. Rush her to E.R! She's not breathing. Her baby is dying!" the medical technician declared.

Oh my God, my baby! My little girl. God, please don't let my baby die. I will change my ways. Lord, spare my child's life and I won't kill her. God, Please. Life for a life.

I promise.

"She's back! She's breathing. Ms. Jones, who did this to you?"

There was only one person egregious enough to pull off this type of act...Alexis Mason.

"Mommy," Kaylah says. "Are you listening to me?"

I snapped out of the nightmare.

"Yes, sweetie. Mommy was hurt a long time ago."

"How?" she innocently asks.

She's not old enough to understand all of the horrific details of a two-year battle with a deranged female stalker.

The threatening phone calls...

The stolen identity...

The false police reports...

The arrests...

The white van...

The gun...

The bomb threats...

The panic attacks...

The court dates...

The lies...

The voodoo...

The fear...

...and the betrayal which made my life a living hell. Twelve years later, I am ready to tell the story.

CHAPTER 1: FRIENDS BEFORE LOVERS

"The only way to have a friend is to be one."
Ralph Waldo Emerson

Your love is wonderful, yeah and I don't want to lose you, So baby, soon as I get home, I'll make it up to you; Baby, I'll do what I gotta do.

I'm sitting at my desk singing Faith Evans' *As Soon As I Get Home*, obviously messing up the words when Marcus comes over and hands me a CD. "What's this?" I asked.

Marcus answers, "It's a Faith Evans cd. You've been torturing the words all week. So I got it for you."

"Wow, that's nice of you. What's your name?"
"Marcus."
"Hi, Marcus. I'm Keacha."
"I know who you are."

A smile appeared on my face. Marcus was a humble and reserved guy. He had a sexy, smart, swag that I liked. His smooth brown skin, thick eyebrows, full lips and dark curly hair, gave him an exotic flair. His clothes were stylish, but fitting. He had no tattoos. The black framed glasses he wore made him look like a businessman. He was a pretty boy, far from the thugs I was used to. Marcus seemed like a nice, respectable guy. Someone I thought I needed in my life.

You see, my life was a roller coaster of ups and downs. The day I can honestly say changed the course of my life was May 16, 1988. I was thirteen years old, and my sister Tinika was about to turn 11. Tinika and I were two years apart, but people often mistook us for twins because my mom dressed us alike.

My sister was my best friend, my confidant, and my partner in crime. We played together, cried together, fought together, and got whoopins' together. Although I had another lil sister Angie, who was five years younger than me, Neek was my best friend.

Tinika and I were tight like glue and tied at the hip. Nothing could tear us apart but death, and on that fateful day of May 16, 1988 everything about my life came to a screeching halt.

One day while Tinika was walking home from school, she collapsed. After being rushed to the hospital and administered series of tests, doctors found out that Tinika had Leukemia. Being only 12 at the time, I didn't know much, if anything, about Leukemia. I never in my wildest dreams thought the person who meant the most to me in the world, would be gone a year later. I always thought my sister would get healthy, and things would turn back to normal.

However, that was not the case. Leukemia had reared its ugly head and turned a very vibrant, energetic and intelligent 11 year old, into an extremely sick little girl. This beast of a disease took a toll on my sister very quickly. Tinika was in and out of the hospital for months receiving chemotherapy treatments, and as a result, her long beautiful thick black hair fell out. Everything in her world was turned upside down.

Tinika could no longer attend school, so a teacher came to our house to tutor her. The once happy go lucky, loving sister I knew, became very sad and mean because of the intense chemotherapy and medication she was given. All I knew was my sister and best friend was not the same person anymore.

Literally, my heart was broken in two, and would never be the same. *How could this be happening to her? Why?* Those were the thoughts racing through my mind on a regular basis. To make matters worse, my mother felt the need to tell Tinika that the man she called daddy all of her life, my father, was not actually her father.

I remember listening outside of my mother's door the day she told her. She showed her a picture of her real dad, but I don't think my mother knew how to get in contact with him or the pain this would cause. I can remember feeling hurt and confused after hearing this. *Why would my mother do this to her? Why was she divulging this kind of information to my sister?* I just didn't understand the reasoning, but one thing did click for me that day. Now it all made sense.

I recalled how my step mother acted towards Tinika whenever we went to visit them. She was always very cold and distant towards her. She would ignore her and act as if she wasn't even there. Tinika never complained or said anything about it, but being protective of my sister, I took notice, and hated my step mother because of it. Tinika didn't deserve that kind of treatment. After all, she was my dad's child too, so I thought.

Leukemia had taken over my family's soul. It tore the life out of everything that we knew as normal. It brought the best, and the worst out of all those who were affected.

The last time my sister went to the hospital, she would not return. She asked the doctors if she could talk to me, but they would not allow her to talk to me nor would they let me talk to her. That very day, she succumbed to that dreadful disease. If you could imagine I was devastated. It felt as though my soul had left with her on that day.

We attended her funeral and the only father she had ever known all those years, My daddy, didn't attend.

After the funeral, everything went back to normal, I guess. The death of my sister affected me like no other. This was the first time I felt real, unbearable pain. Going back to school, everybody said, 'Sorry for your lost, Keacha.'

Sorrrrry. Hmph, I was the one who was sorry. I was sorry my sister had died instead of me. I was sorry I was left alone without my best friend. I didn't go to therapy. I didn't get any counseling, not even at school, or church. Nobody talked about Tinika much. I saw a few pictures of her at my aunt's house, but that was it. She died, and life went on as usual.

After Tinika's death, my mother moved my baby sister, Angie and I into a house with my aunt and two cousins. Although the house was very nice, it was in a poor degraded neighborhood on Lexington Street in Baltimore. Drug addicts and drug dealers plagued the neighborhood. At any moment, you heard voices yelling.

"Yellow top!"
"Red top!"
"Black top!"
"5-0! 5-0!"

Police cars raced through the neighborhood. Like roaches when you turned on the lights, the drug addicts would disappear. It was in this neighborhood that I met Tracy. Tracy became my best friend. She reminded me of the sister I lost, Tinika. She taught me how to stand up for myself, and not let people take advantage of me. She showed me how to dress to impress, and how to do my own hair.

Every day when Tracy and I got off the bus, the neighborhood hustlers, sitting on their front steps, would approach us. Many of them were much older, but all of them were looking for fresh meat. We were divas in the making.

This is when I was nicknamed, Lady. The guys called me Lady, since I wouldn't tell them my real name. My dad also called me Lady, so the name stuck. As a matter of fact, everybody called me Lady, except for my family, who always called me Keacha.

Tracy and I went to Western High School, the top all girls high school in Baltimore City. I was drawn to Tracy because she was the complete opposite of me. I was not confident about my body, she was. I was quiet and timid, Tracy was bold and courageous. She was everything that I wanted to be deep down inside. Little did I know that the relationship we had, would help contribute to the young woman that I would become.

The day I met my son's father, Maurice, I was walking back to church with my three god sisters. I attended New Hope Holiness Church where Sunday service started early in the morning, continued into the afternoon, and was over late at night. This particular Sunday, after the early morning service, my god sisters and I walked to Westside Shopping Center to have dinner at one of the restaurants.

"Hey girl, can I get your number?" I turned around and saw this handsome light-skinned brother.

"Are you talking to me?" I said with a surprised look on my face.

"Yeah," he stated.

By this time my god sisters were blushing and nudging me in the ribs. "He's cute Keacha, get his number." We exchanged numbers and so began my first real relationship.

I really liked Maurice, and cared a lot about him. Maurice accompanied me to my first dance. I would sneak from school to go to his house. I was a virgin, but I wanted to see what all the hype was about. So, Maurice and I started having sex. I didn't think about birth control and condoms. Hell, I didn't think about the fact I could get pregnant. I just did what everyone else was doing. Everyone else didn't get pregnant. I did.

March of 1992, I was sixteen, pregnant and scared. I didn't tell my mother until the summer, when I was almost 4 months pregnant. The next few months of my life were a living hell. My family was ashamed of me because I was the smart girl. I wasn't supposed to get pregnant at sixteen, although my mother had me when she was fifteen.

Nevertheless, my strict upbringing in the holiness church should have taught me not to get pregnant. God was a punisher and surely he would punish me for my bad behavior. After hearing a lecture from all of my aunts, I had to stand in front of the entire congregation, apologize for committing fornication and repent for getting pregnant. Then I was forced to sit on the front pew of the church every Tuesday night, Friday night and both Sunday services, to ensure I was embarrassed to the highest level. I was kicked off of the youth choir, and none of the other girls were allowed to talk to me.

I thought to myself. *What kind of church is this? Why am I apologizing to the church? They are not God.*

How is this going to help me to become a better person? I'm not ashamed of my baby. I'm going to sit here and ignore all of them. All of these girls are having sex. I'm the only one who got caught, so why do I have to wear the scarlet letter S for slut.

My mother had joined this church a few years prior, and they thought that I was trouble before hand. I wasn't any trouble. I just didn't understand how my mother went from a card playing, partying woman to an everyday churchgoing lady. We had never been to a church before then, except for Easter. This surely didn't make any sense to me.

My mother made sure I knew how disappointed she was in me. Looking back on it now, I was just trying to replace something I had lost, love. The love I felt from my sister, Tinika. Since her death, I felt empty with nothing or no one to call my own.

Being pregnant made me feel special. I would have someone to love me and I would love this baby with all my heart. Although I hoped for a girl, I wanted a boy so he could be the big brother for his little sister, I would have one day. When I found out I was having a boy, I was elated. His name would be Dionte'. It was an uncommon name for my very special little boy.

Dionte' was born on December 20, 1992. He was the cutest little baby I had ever seen. Because his father was mixed, Dionte' looked like a little white baby with grey eyes. At first I didn't believe I actually had a baby. I called him *little baby* for a long while, until it kicked in. *This is your son. You are his mommy.* He was the love of my life. He motivated me to do better. I wanted to be the best mother for him. I wanted to give him the life I didn't have. Having Dionte' made me want to make something out of myself.

I knew people had written me off and thought I would be nothing but a welfare mother, so I was determined to prove them wrong. I decided then I would finish high school and go to college to become a teacher.

Considering no one from my family had graduated from college, this would be a great accomplishment for me. It would be tough, but this would help me to become the best mother I could be for my son, and get off of welfare.

I left my mom's house, a few months after I graduated from high school and enrolled in Coppin State College. I could no longer deal with the strict upbringing in the holiness church, and the rules and regulations of the house. My cousin Chanay and I moved into an apartment together. She had a daughter and I had a son, so we thought it was a perfect fit.

This arrangement worked for about a year, until I was hired by the government as a Stay-In-School student. I was ecstatic. I got off of welfare and moved into my own place, separate from my cousin. I was still considered low income, so I qualified for the benefits of daycare vouchers, food stamps, Section 8 vouchers, and medical assistance.

I used the system to my benefit, instead of abusing it.

By the age of 20, I had my own apartment, was in college full-time, and worked part-time. Working for the federal government was a blast. I was mature enough to train the new hires and had a desk, all to myself, unlike the other Stay-In-School students. Many of the guys who worked there were afraid to approach me because I was "intimidating". Always dressed with the latest jeans, a cute top and the hottest stilettos, I brought fashion and style to the building. Besides, I only dealt with hustlers, as far as relationships were concerned. From my appearance, they could tell.

Moving into my own place gave me the freedom and responsibility of an adult. I had a lot of support from my aunts, who watched my son on the weekends. This allowed me time to hang out with my girlfriends, catch up on my school work and date.

Being a product of my environment, I was attracted to thugs and drug dealers. Maybe it was the fact that I didn't have a consistent father figure in my life. Maybe the strength and the style of the hustlers fascinated me. I enjoyed riding around in the fancy cars. I treasured the jewelry, clothes and shoes that were given to me. I loved the fancy restaurants and dates. More so, the access to money anytime I needed it was the icing on the cake.

Growing up poor doesn't leave you with many advantages, so getting cash on a daily basis for being somebody's girl, was like winning the lottery. The glamour and glitz of being the hustler's girl was great, but the fear of getting arrested or visiting someone in jail didn't sit well with me. I promised myself that I would fall in love with a regular guy, get married and live happily ever after, just like in the fairy tales.

In the meantime, I was the girlfriend of Antoine. Originally from New York, Antoine had the block on lock down. Everybody knew he ruled the village and all the hustlers knew I was his girl. Tall and handsome with a New York accent and a bad boy sway, Antoine was the most wanted nigga on every hood chick's list. We met as I was walking home from the bus stop. Antoine yells out the window.

"If you were my girl, you would never have to walk."

"Too bad, I'm not your girl," I responded without looking his way.

"You could be," he said.

"Is that right?" I looked at Antoine and thought to myself, *Damn this nigga is fine*. "Who said I wanna be ya girl?" I asked, playing hard to get.

"You will." He smiled and pulled off. I thought *ain't that some shit. I didn't even get his number.* A few days later, Antoine spotted me again and got out of the car.

"What's up, Ma? When can I take you out?"

"My name is not Ma."

"Well, what's up Lady? When can I take you out?"

"How do you know my name?"

"I know everything, about everybody around here. I'm Antoine. Are you going to be my girl or what?"

We were inseparable after that. Antoine was one of the few men who could handle my feistiness. He had a way of putting my sassy attitude under control, without yelling or hitting. Whatever I wanted, whatever I needed, he provided. I never did walk again. Either I was driving his white BMW 740, or riding in the passenger side.

He loved my son and could have passed as his real father, considering Maurice was out of Dionte's life at the moment. Antoine would pick Dionte' up from school for me on several occasions and hang out with him, until I came home.

Antoine showered me with gifts, shopping and money. He convinced me that as a Lady, I should always wear heals, even with jeans. So off to the mall we went. I had never been shopping where I could pick up anything and everything I wanted. My bags were loaded with Coach, Louis Vuitton and Gucci. I had shirts of every color and shoes to match them all. I had all kinds of jeans, dresses and jewelry, but all that glitters is not gold.

The flashy BMW caused police officers to pull us over on several occasions. A 23 year old black man driving a 7 series BMW in Baltimore was sure to raise attention among the cops. Antoine knew how to talk to the officers and smooth things over each time. Strangely, he knew most of them.

Even hanging out in public was an issue for us. Everywhere we went, girls would stare, roll their eyes, or flirt with him. He loved the attention he got from the women, and the respect he got from the men. Having women in his face all the time was flattering to him. Some women were flat out disrespectful, but they learned quickly that I was not to be disrespected.

Antoine would tell me, "Ma, I know you're not mad, they don't mean nothin' to me. You gonna have to learn how to be tough. Show these bitches who the boss is. I chose you for a reason, Ma. You're tough. Stop letting people walk over you. Handle it."

"Whatever! You handle it," I said with an attitude, rolling my eyes.

"That's your job, Ma. Bitches only gon' do what you allow them to do."

Antoine was right. Some girls took my quietness for weakness and underestimated me. After going off on a few bitches, word got out that I had a bad attitude, and would go off at the drop of a hat. I never got into a physical fight with anyone; I never had to. Game recognized game.

Bitches knew I could handle my own if I had to, but I always remained a lady.

If you don't bother me, I won't bother you. I didn't let petty stuff bother me, but I wasn't going to be blatantly disrespected. I knew how to make bitches feel real small with very few words. I wasn't about all of that shouting and screaming. "All that chirping is for the birds?" I would say. "If you gon' step, bitch step. Otherwise, keep it moving."

Lying in bed one night, my cell phone rings.

"Hello."

"Lady, this is Tasha. I want you to know Antoine is my man now and I don't want you calling him and acting all crazy and shit." This was not the first chick who called my house, but this would be the last.

"Hold on," I said and passed Antoine the phone. *Bitch, please. I can show you better than I can tell you.*

"Hello." Antoine said.

"Antoooooiiinnnne!" I heard the female yell.

"Bitch, what the fuck are you calling my girl for? It ain't shit between us. How did you get this phone number? I will deal with your dumb ass tomorrow. Don't call here again, ever! Do you understand me?"

I never heard from Tasha again. She probably was one of his hoes who stepped out of line, but Antoine didn't take shit off of nobody. He knew how to put things in perspective. I didn't question him. I didn't ask who she was. It didn't matter. The situation was handled.

Me, on the other hand, I wasn't happy with our relationship. I wanted more. I wanted to be romanced. I wanted to walk around the lake, holding hands. As much as Antoine did for me, he was not a romantic. He forgot every holiday, especially Valentine's Day. When I mentioned it, he would throw me five benjamins. Everything was about the money with him.

After two years, I could no longer deal with the fact that I wasn't getting the love that I so desperately wanted. The relationship was in trouble. Eventually, Antoine and I stopped going to the clubs together. I was too close to cutting a few bitches over him, so I decided to hang out with my girlfriends instead.

Tracy, Shawna, and Anecia were my girls. We went to the club every Friday night, leaving the house at midnight and staying until the club closed at six in the morning.

On Saturday mornings, when I arrived at work, my godmother, Ms. Emma would say, "Keacha, where are you coming from?"

"The Paradox," I laughed.

Ms. Emma took me and Marcus under her wings as her adopted children. Ms. Emma worked at SSA for over 20 years. She was the coolest adult I had ever met. I could ask her anything and she would tell me the absolute truth. Little did I know, Marcus had been telling Ms. Emma that he was falling for me and wanted to take our friendship to another level.

Months passed and Marcus and I became very good friends. I never considered Marcus to be the boyfriend type. He had a girlfriend and I had a boyfriend. Most days we would go out for lunch, play spades or just shoot the breeze. We talked a lot on the phone and began hanging out more after work. I still never thought of him as a boyfriend, not until he started saying little things like, "We would have a cute daughter." When he played Usher's song *You Make Me Wanna*, every time I got into his car, I knew Marcus was serious about us.

By this time my relationship with Antoine had grown stale and I had enough. Just so happen, Antoine was caught cheating on me, with my son's pre-school teacher, Ashley. While he was picking up Dionte' from school, he picked up a chick on the side as well.

I was done with Antoine, and Marcus was there to pick up the pieces. The day I was on my way to Ashley's job to fuck her up, Marcus was the one who stopped me. He calmed me down and encouraged me to think about the consequences of my actions. Although he couldn't stop me from destroying Antoine's house, cutting his tires, and bashing out his windows; he convinced me that Antoine didn't deserve me anyway.

Marcus knew Antoine, but he didn't allow that to deter him from being there for me. At the same time, Marcus's girlfriend Peaches, began getting jealous of how close Marcus and I had become. They had just had a son, but it seemed like Marcus wasn't able to groom Peaches into the lady he wanted her to be, so he became frustrated with the relationship.

One day at work, Marcus handed me a book with questions on love and sex. He said, "Read the questions I marked." The questions were all about friends becoming lovers.

I said, "Whoa! That's kind of deep." Marcus was hinting about us taking our friendship a step further. I was kind of interested, so I asked, "Marcus, are you asking me to take our friendship to a new level?"

"Yeah," he answered. "What do you think about that?"

"I don't know, Marcus. I don't think you can handle all of this," I said jokingly while showing off my curves.

"Lady, we've been friends for two years now. I know everything about you. You know everything about me. They say the best lovers are friends, right."

"What about you and Peaches? You just had a baby," I mentioned.

"We broke up," he said.

"Y'all will get back together," I insisted. "I have too much drama in my life for you."

At this time my son was five years old, my younger sister was living with me, and Antoine and I had just broken up. Naturally, I thought that might have been too much for Marcus to consider. It didn't seem to bother him.

"We are like best friends, Lady. You are what I need. Besides we look good together." We both laughed.

"Alright, let's see what happens." I knew a relationship was not going to work out between us. Marcus was not my type. He could not provide me with the lifestyle I had been living for the last two years, but I had to admit to myself, I liked Marcus a lot.

The first time we went out as a couple, I felt like a teenager on her first date. I wore a black, v-cut dress that showed my voluptuous breast and small frame with my favorite Louis Vuitton stilettos, which showcased my beautiful legs. I wanted to show Marcus I could be cool, but sexy. When he arrived at my house holding a bouquet of roses, he couldn't take his eyes off of me.

"Wow, you look nice," Marcus said.

"Thank you," I blushed, as I took the bouquet of roses and sat them on the table, making sure I captured his attention as I walked away.

"So where are we going?"

"We can go to the movies and grab some McDonalds."

"Ok, I will upgrade you after this date," I laughed. "I cooked dinner for you, so we won't be going to McDonald's."

"You did?" Marcus had the brightest smile on his face.

It would be easy to make Marcus into the man I needed. Marcus was mesmerized and I enjoyed being with a good guy. He was different from Antoine. He was quiet, but funny. I could be myself with him and let down my tough girl demeanor. We would laugh and talk on the phone all night. We always had a good time when we were together. We didn't have to put up a front with each other.

Late one evening, Marcus called me. "Lady, I have bad news."

"What happened?" I asked.

"Kim is dead."

"What?" I was delirious. "What are you talking about? I just talked to Kim a little while ago at work. You shouldn't play like that!"

"Lady, she's dead. Her boyfriend stabbed her nineteen times."

"What, she's in a wheelchair! How could he stab her nineteen times?"

My heart was heavy for Kim. Kim was like a big sister to me. She was nineteen years old, when she was accidentally shot by her brother and paralyzed. Nevertheless, Kim remained positive and took care of her two children, while working at

SSA, where we became friends. She always had a smile on her face and kept me laughing.

Unfortunately, Kim met an insane, possessive guy, who wouldn't leave after the relationship was over. Instead, he waited in the dark corner of her apartment and stabbed her to death. Such was life in the hood. This was the second time; I experienced death close to me. My sadness over Kim's death brought Marcus and I closer. He kept close watch on me and made sure I was ok.

I was starting to think I could be Marcus' girlfriend. With him, I felt safe. I could let go of the drama that came with being the girlfriend of a hustler. No more crazy girls calling my house. No more hoping the police officer didn't pull over the white BMW. No more bitches rolling their eyes, when I'm out with my man. No more cheating. I finally had a good guy and I was going to keep him.

Giving up my hustler's girl lifestyle also meant that I gave up my hustler's girl money. I had to depend on my own finances to support my lifestyle and things got really tough for me financially. I put all of my furniture in storage and moved in with Tracy for a little while. My sister had moved across town with her father, and this would give me an opportunity to save up some money. After a short stay with Tracy, Marcus and I moved into a townhouse together.

Marcus had never been on his own, so he didn't have furniture and credit to purchase items for the house. All of the furniture was mine and all the bills were in my name. Living together increased the intensity in our relationship. We never argued. We talked about our dreams and what we envisioned our life to be like.

I would wake up to Marcus preparing me breakfast in bed, almost every Saturday morning. In the evenings, he would lay a blanket on the floor and fix us a delicious dinner with champagne. On occasion, Marcus would arrange our bedroom with rose petals on the bed and light candles around the room. He would make me a hot bubble bath, and then give me a full body massage.

I was completely spoiled by Marcus. Our sexual chemistry was unbelievable. I had never had a man like Marcus, whose main concern was to make me happy without anything in return. I was falling for Marcus hard. He was my king and I was his queen.

Although we worked together and lived together, we didn't get tired of each other. We didn't want our co-workers to know we were in a relationship, so we would sneak through different doors and sign in a few minutes apart. They soon figured out what was going on, especially Ms. Emma. She was excited that we had gotten together and were blissfully in love. Throughout the day, I caught Marcus staring at me and I would smile in response. Everything was perfect. I was getting the romance I had yearned for all my life.

That year, Marcus and I celebrated our first Christmas as a couple. We had so much fun bringing our kids together as a blended family. I wanted to show Marcus how much he meant to me at Christmas. I bought him a pair of Sean Jean jeans, a Coogi sweater and a pair of Timberland boots. I was skeptical about buying boots because my grandmother always said, 'If you buy a man shoes, he will walk out of your life.' That was an old wives tales because there was no way Marcus was leaving me.

For my Christmas gift, Marcus bought me a yellow North Face ski jacket, a jean Gucci outfit and a giant teddy bear. We spent the entire day together visiting our families.

After a few months, Marcus told me he wanted to talk. "Oh, boy," I said. "What's wrong?" Although we were in a relationship, it was important that we remained friends and kept the lines of communication open.

"I want my own place," he responded.

"You do. Why?"

"I've never lived on my own. I feel like this is all yours. I want to know how it feels to be independent."

"So what's going to happen to us?"

"Nothing, we are still a couple. We would live in separate houses, but that would make the relationship even more exciting. I can sneak over here at night and seduce you," he said, trying to make me feel better about his decision.

"Okay," I said sadly. "If that's what you want. I want you to be happy." I put on a fake smile. Things were changing at that point.

Marcus moved in January. I hoped he would reconsider, since I was leaving my job to complete student teaching, an unpaid internship. I would not have an income for 12 weeks to help me pay the bills. Nevertheless, he moved out.

Marcus' choice of apartment bothered me more than his actual moving. He moved into an apartment that he and Peaches had planned on moving into. The apartment was located directly across the street from Peaches' house, but 45 minutes away from me.

One day, Shawna, called me. She saw Marcus and Peaches walking around the shopping center together. I called his cell phone; he didn't answer. I was furious. I couldn't believe Marcus was trying to play me. I thought...

I can't believe this nigga is trying to play me. Does he know who the fuck I am? He is sadly mistaken, if he thinks I'm about to sit here, while he tries to put his family back together with his baby mama. How does he think he's going to play me and not have any consequences? I'm about to fuck his ass up.

I was so hurt and angry. I didn't think it could be a simple get together or outing. I was known to fly off the handle and this time Marcus was the target instead of the comforter.

I packed up everything Marcus left at my house, called Tracy and Shawna, and we all headed to Marcus' apartment. His car was not in the parking lot, but I still banged on his apartment door, hoping that he and Peaches were in the apartment. I stormed back to my car and got all of his things. I threw his clothes all over the apartment building, wrote Bitch Marcus on big pieces of paper and taped them all over the building.

I was furious. I had allowed Marcus to let me become emotionally weak and dependent on him. I trusted him and assumed we were happy together, but then realized he was the same as all the other guys I had dealt with.

On his way home, Marcus called me and tried to explain what was going on. I started yelling, "Nigga, you're trying to play me! Fuck you!" And hung up the phone.

When he arrived at the building, he called again. "What the fuck did you do this for? Are you out of your damn mind? Bitch Marcus! Oh, I'm a bitch now? You're so damn evil, you won't even listen. There is nothing going on with Peaches and me. I took her to get some stuff for my son."

I could hear a crack in his voice. He was angry and hurt. I felt like an asshole and immediately regretted my actions. I allowed my emotions to get the best of me. I reacted first and asked questions last. I tried to justify my behavior by saying, he should have answered the damn phone, but inside I hated what I had done. I hurt the only man that I had loved.

It was more important for me to get even, than it was to wait and talk to him about what was happening. I messed up big time with Marcus. He couldn't forgive me for overreacting. We broke up and went our separate ways. He started seeing other girls, and I went back to Antoine.

Ms. Emma called me to give updates of Marcus' life. "Lady, you know he still loves you."

Marcus called me every once in a while, but he never visited or asked me out again. Despite our breakup, Marcus attended my college graduation in May.

College graduation was a big deal for me. After five years of school work, taking care of my son, looking after my sister and moving a couple of times, I accomplished the goal I set out to do. I graduated with a Bachelor of Science Degree in Education. I was the first person in my family to hold the title, college graduate. Yep me, a teenage mother at the age of 17, graduated with a 3.6 average. Everyone was proud. All of my family, including my father and my stepmother, came to my graduation. It was a very special day for me and Marcus was there to share it.

In August, I began my career as an elementary school teacher. I worked at one of the best schools in Baltimore City, with an extraordinary principal. Mr. Smith offered me a job immediately after I completed student teaching. My first year of teaching, I taught second grade. Becoming a teacher calmed me down. I wanted to be a positive role model to my students, as well as my son. I desired to leave the hood life behind, but I didn't know how to break up with Antoine again.

As I was riding home with Antoine thinking about how I can break up with him peacefully, the police pulled us over.

"Oh shit!" Antoine stated.

"What? What?" I asked, frantically. We had been pulled over several times before and it never was a problem.

"I'm dirty. It's five kilos in the trunk!"

My life was over. I could see my face on the Channel 2 News.

"Be calm," he said.

Calm, nigga please. I am not meant for jail. Luckily for us, the police officer let him go, again. I had never seen Antoine so nervous in my life. At that moment, we both knew that our time was up. As much as Antoine loved me, he loved the street life more. He wasn't giving it up for me and he could no longer jeopardize my safety and the life I had built for myself and my son.

I had a career, not just a job and I refused to be on the news, under the headline, *Baltimore City*

Teacher Caught with 5 Kilos of Cocaine. Besides, I was still in love with Marcus and no one could make me feel the way he made me feel.

Antoine and I said our goodbyes, promising if we needed anything, we would always be there for each other. I was ready to be independent. I had made it out of the ghetto, out of the hood and was ready for the new life that was ahead of me. With or without Marcus, I was determined to be happy. I was single, but not desperate. I needed time to focus on Keacha and Dionte'. No men. No drama.

CHAPTER 2: A LOVE TRIANGLE

"The saddest thing in the world is loving someone who used to love you."
Anonymous

Because it was a new millennium, the year 2000; everyone was afraid there would be a universal computer system shutdown or that the world would disappear. I decided if the world was going to collapse, I would be home with my son on New Year's Eve. 12:00 midnight came. HAPPY NEW YEAR! There was a blackout. After a brief period, the lights flashed on. My son and I jumped around and cheered. The world did not collapse. We were still alive. My pager beeped. Marcus had left a message: "Happy New Year!"

I made the decision to move out of Baltimore City, and moved to Chase, Maryland. I found a nice, new townhouse in Benoni Circle, which was much cheaper than my townhouse in the city. Besides, I wanted a change of environment. I had a new career and a new look on life. My next goal was to save money to buy a house in the upcoming year.

Marcus and I had been broken up for about a year and a half. He called every now and then, and told me about things going on in his life, in particular his new girlfriend, Alexis. She reminded him of me with her independence, but she was depressed a lot, he mentioned. She suffered from manic depression and bi-polar disorder.

Damn! I thought.

According to Marcus, he met Alexis at the club, where she worked as a stripper. He was excited about her persistently pursuing him, until she got pregnant, a month later. Marcus told Alexis that he was not ready for another baby, because his son was only three. They started having problems. Alexis had a miscarriage and lost their baby.

Ms. Emma called me sounding troubled, "Lady, you better talk to Marcus. This new girl is trouble. He is not happy. He mopes around at work, complaining about her. She calls him all day, even when he hangs up on her, she calls right back."

"Really? He told me a little bit about her, but not much. I think my cousin used to date the same girl. I will talk to him about her," I assured Ms. Emma.

"Hey, Cool. Do you know Alexis Mason?"

"Yeah, that was the crazy girl that got me arrested."

"What?" I exclaimed. "The girl that used to fight you all the time."

"Yes, that's her. Why, what's up? Y'all friends?"

"Naw. Marcus is dating her now."

"Keacha, tell Marcus to leave her alone. There is a lot he don't know about her," Cool sounded concerned.

"Really? Like what?"

"For one, she is crazy as hell!" yelled Cool. "She was in a mental hospital on several occasions. If she doesn't take her medicine, she goes off and starts fighting people, throwing things and having these violent tantrums."

"Cool, are you serious?" I asked, getting worried for Marcus.

"Yes!" he stated. "Alexis would be fine, happy and cheerful one minute. The next minute, she would go completely crazy. She would get depressed, wouldn't comb her hair, wouldn't go to work or take care of her daughter. Her mother takes care of her daughter most of the time."

I was shocked. "I can't believe Marcus would get involved with someone like this."

"He probably got fooled like I did. When I first met her, she was sweet. I told her I wasn't looking for a relationship on several occasions, but she had other plans. She was in love and I was in lust. She thought she could change my mind.

She started getting too clingy, so I began distancing myself. All hell broke loose then. She made it her personal mission to make my life a living hell and that's when the fighting started. She would pop up over my house. When I asked her to leave, she became violent. She started fighting, screaming, and knocking over shit.

The last time she came over uninvited, this other chick was over here. She went ballistic. They started fighting. I called the police, but the officer took me to jail. The next day, she called crying hysterically and apologizing. Finally, I kept ignoring her and she stopped coming around."

"Probably, because she found Marcus. I'll tell Marcus what you said Cool, but he won't believe me," I said. "How long did y'all date?"

"All this happened over three months."

"What! That's crazy as hell!"

"Yeah! Those were the worst three months of my life. She is desperate for a man and will go to any means necessary to keep one. Tell Marcus to call me. I will keep it real with him. That girl is psychotic." Cool said.

"Is she prettier than me?" I asked.

"Hell no!" said Cool.

I smiled and ended the call. Of course Cool would say Alexis was not prettier than me. He's my big cousin. That's what he's supposed to say.

I called Marcus to tell him what Cool said about Alexis. "Yeah, I know she has problems," Marcus said.

"Then why are you with her?"

"At first, she reminded me of you. She seemed to be independent and had a lot going for herself. Like you, she goes to school. She works. She takes care of her daughter. I thought we would be good together. Then she started acting crazy. You remember when you popped off on me at the apartments?"

"Yeah," I regretfully stated.

"She's like that, but every other day she's popping off about one thing or another. I never know what's going to set her off."

"Why don't you break up with her?"

"I've tried. I have done everything humanly possible to break up with her. She starts crying uncontrollably and tells me she will kill herself."

"What are you going to do?"

"I don't know, but I know that I miss you, Lady." Marcus changed the subject.

"You do?" I asked excitingly.

"Yeah, I wish I'd called you that day and worked it out with you. I wish I had answered the phone and told you there was nothing going on between Peaches and me. She was trying to get back with me, but I wasn't interested in her anymore. I didn't know how you would handle me being out with her, so I ignored the call. When I got to the apartment and saw where you had written Bitch Marcus all over the place, I was hurt. I thought we were better than that. I didn't know how to come to you after that."

"I'm sorry, Marcus." I said in a sweet low tone. "I really didn't mean to hurt you. After the incident, I realized I was wrong and needed to think about my actions first and not after the damage. Do you forgive me?"

"Of course, I forgive you, baby. You're my soul mate."

"You think so?" I asked.

"I know so. I think about you all the time. I still have your clothes in my dresser. I ask Ms. Emma about you every day. I pray for you at night and hope you will come back to me."

We sat on the phone silently, content that we found our way back to each other.

Marcus started driving out to Chase to see me. A few weeks later, his car's transmission broke, so he stayed with me until his car was fixed. Our jobs were not far from each other, so sharing a car wasn't a problem. Our feelings started growing for each other again.

He had broken up with Alexis and began distancing himself, but she wasn't taking it very well. She continued to call his cell phone cussing him out and leaving him threatening messages. Marcus told me he needed money to take care of something. I figured Alexis was telling him she was pregnant again and wanted an abortion. I said to myself, 'Marcus and I belong together. Let that bitch get an abortion, so we can move on with our lives.'

That was the beginning of our new relationship. We started dating again and taking the children out together as a family. He attended all of my son's baseball games and stayed at my house almost every evening.

For Valentine's Day Marcus ordered steak from Ruth Chris Steakhouse and surprised me with a romantic dinner at home. The following weekend, he planned a ski trip to the Poconos for us.

As we were driving to the bus station, we heard a Boom! A jeep slammed into the back of my car. "What the hell?" I yelled, jumping out of the car, ready to pop off again. "I know you did not slam into the back of my brand new mutha fuckin' car!"

Marcus stopped me. "Lady, I got it. Calm down. Get back in the car."

The young white guy who was driving looked petrified. Marcus called our friends to let them know we would miss the bus. He completed the police report, contacted the insurance company and got the directions to Pennsylvania. I loved the way he took control of the situation.

"You need to stop going off on people," Marcus said.

"Well, he should not have hit my damn car," I responded.

"What if he was sick and lost control?" he asked.

"What if I was sick and whooped his ass?" We both started laughing.

The entire drive we talked about our relationship.

Marcus told me how we belonged together, and no one compared to me. He assured me that he was going to fix "his situation" so that we could be together.

The Poconos trip gave us a better opportunity to enjoy each other. We indulged in shopping, eating and drinking. Each evening we went dancing at the nightly parties. I didn't know how to skate, so Marcus taught me. It was a perfect weekend.

Going back to Baltimore brought on depressing feelings for Marcus. The trip coming back was much quieter than the trip going. I could sense that Marcus wasn't telling me everything I needed to know about his relationship with Alexis. *What I didn't know wouldn't hurt me or would it?*

A few weeks later, Marcus came to my house. "We need to talk," he said.

"Not again!" I laughed. "What is it this time? You want to move out again? Oh wait, you don't live with me," I teased.

"Alexis is pregnant." The smile vanished from my face.

"Really, Marcus? Is she pregnant or is she saying that to get you to come back to her?"

"No, she is really pregnant. I saw the test and went with her to the doctor's appointment."

"And you thought that you should wait until now to tell me? How long have you known?"

"She told me a few weeks ago, but I wanted to confirm it today before I mentioned it to you. Things have been good between us and I didn't want to bring it up unnecessarily."

"Is she keeping it?"

"Yes, I told her I didn't want a baby right now. I told her that she and I were not in a good place to have a child together, but she insists that she wants the baby."

"Of course she does. What do you want me to do?" I asked.

"What do you want to do? I will understand if you don't want us to be together anymore. I still hope that we can remain friends, if that's your decision."

"I will think about it," I said. I was not leaving Marcus, but I didn't know how I would deal with two baby mamas. Peaches, his first child's mother, had moved on with her life. However, everything about Alexis seemed to be trouble. I had never met her, but I had bad vibes about this girl. I asked myself, 'Am I willing to put up with drama from Alexis to be with Marcus?'

Secretly, I wished I was pregnant instead of Alexis. On the other hand, there was no sense of taking a chance in both of us being pregnant, so I immediately made an appointment to get birth control pills. Previously, I had the Norplant, a birth control device in my arm for five years. It had been removed about two years ago, but I had not become pregnant; although Marcus and I had unprotected sex. I really didn't think I could get pregnant again, but it was better to be safe than sorry.

On my 25th birthday, Marcus placed a rose, a card, and a book in my car while I was at work. After work, we went to dinner and had a nice evening. His birthday was a week away, and I would be in the Bahamas with Tracy, Shawna, and Anecia, so I took Marcus out to dinner. I also planned to bring him a gift back from my trip. As I was leaving to board the plane, I told Marcus that I loved him. Strangely, he didn't respond.

The fact that Marcus didn't return my words of affection bothered me the entire trip, but I tried to put it out of my head. On top of that, I spent most of the time trying to figure out how I was going to tell him, I was pregnant.

While I was waiting for my period to start the birth control pills, it never came. I ran to Rite Aid to buy a pregnancy test. Sure enough, the pink positive sign appeared. I was pregnant. Although I was excited, I knew this would be trouble for Marcus: two women pregnant at the same time, three months apart.

I called Marcus every day during my trip, but didn't get any responses. His birthday was that Sunday and I wanted to wish him a Happy Birthday. He didn't answer.

"What are you going to do, Lady? He's got that other girl pregnant," Tracy stated.

"I don't care. I can take care of my own baby."

"But Lady, you deserve better than that," said Shawna. "You said you would wait until you got married to have another baby."

"Married. Who the hell does that?" I asked. Hardly anyone I knew was married. Besides, all of the married people I knew were unhappy.

"You also said you would not have a bunch of different last names on your mailbox. Remember that?" Anecia asked.

"Yeah," I said. One of my biggest irritations was seeing a mailbox with the mother's name and five kids, all with different last names underneath. I promised myself I would not be that person. I was supposed to be married the next time I got pregnant. Things don't always happen like you plan.

"So you are going to settle being baby mama number three?" asked Tracy.

"I guess so," I regretfully stated.

"Didn't you say that bitch was crazy?" asked Anecia. Before I could speak, Tracy said. "She ain't that crazy! We would take a bitch out by any means necessary."

We all started laughing. I loved my girls. They were always there for me, no matter what. I understood their point of views, but I wanted this baby. My son was almost eight and I wanted a daughter.

Marcus picked me up from the airport. I was delighted to see him, but I kept the pregnancy a secret until I confirmed it at the doctors, the following day. After getting confirmation, I was indeed pregnant; I called Marcus.

"You are not going to be happy about this, but this is my decision and I'm doing what's best for me."

"What are you talking about?"

"I'm pregnant," I said quickly.

"Oh, my God, two babies!" he yelled. "Two babies! What the hell?" Marcus was obviously upset.

"This is not your problem. This is my problem," I insisted.

"I thought you were getting on the pill."

"I was supposed to start this month, but my period didn't come."

"On my fucking God, what am I going to do? I bet you told everybody, huh?"

"No, I called you after I spoke with the doctor's office."

"I don't think you should tell anybody about this until you are about five months."

"Five months, Marcus? Why?" I asked.

"You don't know what might happen. I thought you couldn't get pregnant."

"Me too."

"Are you sure this is something you want to do? I was satisfied with one child, unhappy about Alexis and now you. This shit is too much!" Marcus snapped.

"You know what, you should have thought about that before you were fucking two girls at the same time." I was about to go off on Marcus. "You think I asked for this? I was minding my own damn business when you eased your way back into my life. Now all of a sudden, it's all about you. Fuck you Marcus. Like I said, it's not your problem. I will take care of it."

At that point I knew I wouldn't mention the pregnancy to Marcus anymore. He couldn't take care of two baby mamas. Unfortunately, I would have to face this pregnancy alone, but I was still excited. I told my mother, my family, and all my friends.

Marcus started isolating himself from me, but came to visit the Friday night before Mother's Day. He left Saturday morning. Everything seemed fine, so it was odd that he didn't call or answer the phone when I called. After several attempts of trying to reach him, I thought he might be at Alexis' house. I didn't know exactly where she lived, but I knew the apartments were called Tree Crest. They were ten minutes away from my house. I drove to the apartments, praying that I wouldn't see his car. I was flabbergasted when I saw his car.

I was so angry. I didn't know what to do. Immediately, crazy thoughts ran through my head, but I refused to make a scene outside. I didn't know her exact apartment, so I couldn't run up in there. Furthermore, I was pregnant; I was in no condition to fight. With no other sensible options, I placed a note on Marcus' windshield that read, *I'm waiting for you to call me back.*

I convinced myself that he was taking Alexis a card because of Mother's Day, so I waited in the car. After two and a half hours, I left. I'm sure he gave her more than a card.

The next afternoon, Marcus called and said, "Happy Mother's Day. That's all I had to say." The phone slammed.

Hurt could not describe the pain I was feeling. He used me, played me, and deceived me; yet he was supposed to be my best friend. I wanted to know if he had sex with her. I knew he had, but I wanted to hear him to say it. I called his cell phone again.

"Marcus, what the fuck is going on? Are you back with Alexis now? Are you fucking her?" I yelled irrationally. He didn't respond and hung up the phone. I continued to call Marcus phone back to back. He continued to hang up. This went on all day.

That night I could not sleep. I cried so much, I started cramping and thought I would miscarry. I continued to call him. He continued to ignore me. *He doesn't care. If one baby was dead, it would be better than him having two babies.*

I was pregnant and hopeless. I called again that Monday morning before he went to work and he answered. "Lady, you need to stop calling me like that," he said, sounding annoyed.

"Marcus, what the fuck is going on? You slept with me on Friday, and then slept with her on

Saturday. What kind of shit is that?" I stated angrily.

"Technically, Lady, I'm not with either of you. We are just friends."

"Just friends! So now we're just friends!" I yelled.

"Actually, I'm going back with Alexis. I want you and I to be *just* friends."

The words hurt like a dagger in my heart. I was in tears. I could not figure out what went wrong. I thought everything was fine. I felt so foolish. Marcus had played me again. Maybe his purpose in my life was to get back at me for breaking up with him a long time ago. I couldn't understand what triggered the sudden change of heart. I was the stupid one, getting pregnant when I knew he already had someone else pregnant.

Two weeks later, Marcus shows up on my job with a letter and a dozen of roses, apologizing for his actions. His letter stated that he wanted us to remain friends. He also wanted to be a part of the baby's life. He knew I was disappointed in him, but he didn't know how to make the situation better. He mentioned that he was not with Alexis. At this point, I didn't know what to believe.

The school year ended, so I took Dionte' to South Carolina for the summer to stay with my aunt. I asked Marcus to check on my house while I was gone. I arrived home that Sunday night, only to find three urgent messages from Marcus stating that Alexis was going to call me. Apparently, she saw his car at my house and started questioning him about our relationship. Marcus continued to deny the relationship with her. He convinced me that he wasn't hiding anything else.

The next morning, I was talking with Marcus on the phone when Alexis called. I clicked over to the other line to talk with her.

"Keacha, this is Alexis. I need to speak with you about Marcus." She didn't call me Lady, like everyone else. "Did you know Marcus and I were back together and I'm six months pregnant?"

"Yes, Alexis. I know that you are pregnant, but Marcus told me, you two are not an item."

"Honey, we are together. I found out he was staying over your house while you were out of town."

"How do you know where I live?" I asked.

"Marcus told me," she replied.

"Marcus and I were together while you were in the Bahamas for your birthday. We are going to make our relationship work. He told me that you were dull, and he didn't want to be with you anymore. We agreed he wouldn't have anything to do with you, until you had the baby."

"WE? So why was Marcus at my house again?" I asked sarcastically. This bitch was starting to piss me off. "Hold on. Let me call him," I said. I clicked over to Marcus and put him on the three-way.

"Marcus, you need to let your lil girlfriend know, it is over between y'all," she said. I was about to interrupt, but to my surprise, Marcus snapped.

"Alexis, how many times do I have to tell you I DO NOT want to be with you? I left Lady to try and make it work with you. I wanted you to see it wasn't going to work between us, but you can't see that. You and I don't get along. We argue all the time. You have this delusion in your mind that we are a perfect couple. I can't take you anymore. I want us to be buddies. I will take care of the baby, but you and I are not an item."

Alexis paid Marcus absolutely no attention and focused her concentration back to me, "Keacha, Marcus and I are going to be together no matter what. Both of our pregnancies were planned and we are a family." I snickered, Alexis continued. "What kind of woman are you to get pregnant by a man who already had someone else pregnant? If you are really pregnant, that is the oldest trick in the book."

"Alexis, don't get it twisted sweetheart. I've known Marcus for five years. You on the other hand, were pregnant one month after you met him. Now what kind of woman are you? Oh, but I guess that's what strippers do, right?" She sighed, getting irritated, but I kept talking. "When Marcus came crawling back to me, I did not know that you were pregnant. He eventually told me; however, I was already pregnant. I do not need Marcus to take care of my child. Unlike you, I take care of my own. Marcus doesn't have to do shit for me, boo. I have a career. I have a house. I have a car. Best believe, I am fine. Furthermore, I do not have time for this drama you both are bringing to my life, and I do not have time for these lil girl games. You can have Marcus, sweetie. Obviously, you need him more than I do."

"No bitch, you want him, but I got him," she responded.

"Bitch, who the fuck are you talking to? I'm trying to talk to you like a woman, but you got some fuckin' nerves calling my mutha' fuckin' house talking shit. If you had him, then he would not have been coming over to my house fuckin' me, would he? If you had him, he would not have been traveling with me to other states, would he? If you had him, we wouldn't be having this conversation right now, would we? So you can go ahead with that bull shit."

"It sounds like you have venom in your voice," Alexis retorted. "I heard about you, Miss Keacha. I know how you get down. Yeah, I used to date your cousin, Cool. Your ex-boyfriend Antoine and I are good friends. He told me all about your lil attitude. You think you all that, but bitch you ain't shit. You don't want to see me."

"Lil girl, I don't give a fuck what Antoine told you. Fuck him and fuck you, too. Do I want to see you? Bitch, please! You called me, begging me not to fuck your man. If you were half the woman you think you are, you would be here in my face, not on the fuckin' phone. As far as I am concerned, I'm giving you Marcus. This lil phone thing is not going to happen again. If you feel it will be a problem between us, say the word BITCH, and I will have the problem taken care of instantly. Since you know how I get down, then you know that I don't play games with bitches or niggas. I don't make empty promises or idle threats. This conversation is over and don't dial my mutha fuckin' number again!" I hung up the phone.

I needed to go straight gangster on Alexis. I had to make it clear that I did not have time for her games, nor would I tolerate her harassing me. Pregnant or not, I was not a punk. I tried to lose my tough girl behavior and change my ways, but the hood always has a way of dragging you back in. The guilt I felt after vandalizing Marcus' building made me change my conduct and grow up. I stopped cussing people out and acting irrational. I moved away from Baltimore City to get away from that drama. Now drama was knocking on my door, and I was not about to be intimidated by a psycho, bi-polar bitch.

Alexis was not the first female who called me about some nigga. Usually after a tongue lashing, the conversation was over. No other female attempted to call me back or take matters any further. In my mind, this was this end of the drama. In Alexis mind, this was just the beginning.

After I hung up, Marcus immediately called back, begging me to give him another chance. He said that everything was in the open now and this wouldn't happen again.

Later that evening, I went to Marcus house to get my keys, but he wouldn't give them back. In my heart, I really didn't want them back. *He stood up for me and told Alexis that he didn't want to be with her. He's serious this time.*

His family still didn't know that I was pregnant, which bothered me, but I didn't say anything. Marcus suggested we go to my favorite restaurant, Olive Grove to get something to eat. On the way to the restaurant, he played Sisqo's song, *If It Is Love*, and kept apologizing.

I told him I had a date with my ex, Antoine. Marcus did not want to hear about me getting back with Antoine. So he got on his knees and begged for forgiveness. I forgave him again, not knowing this would only be a test, for the forgiveness I would eventually have to find.

Marcus hadn't been to my house since the conversation with Alexis. He was tired of driving out that far, was his excuse. It was obvious he didn't want Alexis to see his car at my house. On the Fourth of July, he drove me to South Carolina to pick up my son. He met my family and we spent a lot of time together.

We returned to Baltimore only to find Alexis had called my house about thirty times each day. Marcus denied it was her calling. Who else would call my house thirty times a day from NAME/NUMBER UNKNOWN and not leave a message?

I had never seen Alexis in person, but the pictures I saw confirmed how unattractive she was. Regardless, Marcus was still infatuated with her. He tried to convince me Alexis was depressed because she had lost her job as a correctional officer; so he was concerned about the baby. I could not shake the feeling that he was still hiding something.

Around this time, Marcus' secret about me being pregnant came out. It didn't matter. He showed no interest in my pregnancy. By August, I had bought everything the baby needed by putting it on layaway. I told Marcus he could give me half of the money for the layaway, but he didn't.

It seemed as if he wanted a competition between Alexis and me. He went to all of Alexis' doctor's appointments; he went to none of mine. He bought Alexis' baby clothes, shoes and toys. He bought nothing for my baby. If I showed him clothes and furniture I bought for our baby; he would say nonchalantly, "Oh, that's nice."

Alexis found out I was having a girl and she went crazy. She told Marcus she needed six hundred dollars to go to New York, where she could get an abortion at six months pregnant. She didn't want both of us having a girl, but she, nor did Marcus have six hundred dollars for an abortion; so she started taking pills in an effort to kill her baby.

The phone calls continued to my house from NAME/NUMBER UNKNOWN. Marcus continued to insist it wasn't her calling me. One particular day, her name, Alexis Mason, actually appeared on my caller ID. She obviously forgot to press *67 on her phone. I called Marcus and said, "Alexis Mason came up on my caller ID."

He yelled, "What kind of games is she playing? I will call you back."

A few minutes later, someone knocked on the door. I opened the door to find a light-skinned girl with a baby in her arms.

"May I use your phone? I'm locked out of my house," she said. I thought. *She must be a neighbor.* I allowed her use the phone. As I'm listening, she says, "I'm in here."

She left and walked across the parking lot, behind the other townhomes. *Why did she pass all of those houses to use my phone?* I immediately called Marcus and described the girl to him. He said the girl I described seemed like Alexis' friend, Tammy. From then on, I knew Alexis was crazy for real and I had better start watching my back.

A few days later, my sister Angie, called. "Please tell me the ugly girl I saw Marcus with, is not his baby mama."

"What? You saw Marcus? Where?"

"At the airport."

Marcus was with Alexis, picking up her family from Trinidad. I couldn't understand why he kept going back and forth between us. I called him to see what was going on. He said, "Alexis will probably be calling you again."

"Why?" I asked.

"I love both of y'all, but I couldn't sleep with you both, so I chose her," was his response.

By now, I was tired of being humiliated by Marcus. I was tired of being lied to, tired of him slapping me in my face, and tired of him putting Alexis ahead of me. Five years of friendship, and now I was having his baby and I was the one being mistreated.

I broke down and told my mother everything that was happening. I couldn't carry this pain and hurt by myself anymore. I needed some moral support from someone who loved me unconditionally.

I had so many unanswered questions. *Why me? Why would my best friend treat me like this? We talked about everything. We were perfect together. Why does he intentionally hurt me? Did he know I had feelings, too? Did he care? Did he really love me? Is this love?*

In my mind, Marcus got pleasure out of making me cry. It was his mission to make me miserable. I tried to stay strong. I tried to move on. He kept writing me letters, sending me emails, and apologizing. He had only known Alexis for one year, so I couldn't understand the strong attachment he had to her. I suspected she put voodoo on him or had someone else to put it on him.

I had heard stories of people from the islands putting voodoo on men to keep them and to make them fall in love with them. If this was true, then I was a witness to some real voodoo shit. Marcus was a little pitiful puppy to whatever Alexis said. He couldn't seem to shake her. And I couldn't seem to shake him.

I told Marcus I didn't want anything else to do with him. I got my keys back, blocked his number from my phone, and said goodbye. About a week later, he was at my school again, bringing me lunch, along with the saddest note I'd ever read. Again, apologizing and asking me not to shut him out of my life and to give him another chance.

Why did I continue falling for his tricks? I wanted us to be a couple so bad. I wanted him to see how much I was hurting. I needed him to make it right.

Dealing with Marcus and Alexis would eventually drive me crazy, so I distanced myself as much as possible. I occupied my time by looking for a house to purchase.

Marcus' daughter was born on September 11, 2000. As soon as, his little girl was born, he excitedly called me from the hospital. "Congratulations." I said half heartedly. I had to muster up all the strength that was ever in me to just mutter those words. I was thinking, *Why in the hell is he telling me? What the hell do I care about that situation?*

The next day, he asked me if I could meet him at his mother's house because we needed to talk. I went over to his mother's house and he put on the biggest performance ever. He took out pictures of us together and said, "If you can walk away from all of this, I will never bother you again. I tried to make it work with Alexis. Now that the baby is born, I know it won't work," he insisted. "I'm trying to make the best of the situation, but I am very unhappy. I hoped Alexis would see that a relationship wasn't going to work between us and break up with me, but she won't. I'm in love with you. I want us to be together. If you tell me this day you don't want me, I will leave you alone."

Marcus didn't realize how much damage he had done to me. I lifted him above other men. He was supposed to be different and better, but he treated me worse than any man I had been with…all because I allowed him. I kept going back to him. I kept trying to work it out. I wanted to be all he needed. I wanted him to stop playing games with Alexis and be with me, where he belonged.

Marcus knew that I would always be available, especially since I was pregnant by him. He thought he could play around long enough to fix the situation and I would take him back. That's a game I allowed him to play with me. Our relationship wasn't the best, but I still wouldn't let him go. I thought I needed a man to be happy. I thought I needed Marcus.

Alexis only got pregnant to keep Marcus in her life. Just like my cousin, Cool said, she was desperate for a man. I couldn't help but wonder, *Why would she get pregnant by someone she had only been dating one month? Then again, how could I get pregnant by someone who already had another girl pregnant? Maybe I got pregnant to keep him also.* I was just as desperate as Alexis. I was so embarrassed and ashamed. I was played like a piano. Me…. tough girl….. sassy mouth…… hard-core…. Lady….. PLAYED.

CHAPTER 3: DEATH THREATS

"Above all things, never be afraid. The enemy who forces you to retreat is himself afraid of you at that very moment."
Andre Maurois

Instead of focusing on the drama of Marcus and Alexis, I focused my attention on my job. In my previous two years as a teacher, I was deemed a fascinating teacher by my principal. He would often bring visitors to my classroom to watch me teach or demonstrate lessons.

Being a mentor for the other new teachers, I showed them how to set up their classrooms, put behavior management plans in place, and improve their teaching strategies. At Mr. Smith's request, I was highlighted on Action 2 News to speak about the challenges of being a new teacher in Baltimore City. This caused jealousy with some of the younger teachers.

In the fall of 2000, I was excited to be teaching 2nd grade again for my third year. I was going on maternity leave in December, so I prepared my students early, by setting the standards of my classroom. My son was in third grade at the school where I taught, so it was easier for me to commute to work, without worrying about daycare and after school programs.

After school, I made use of my time by looking for a new house. Each day the realtor took me to different homes in Northeast Baltimore, where I wished to live. I needed to be closer to my family, but was adamant about living outside of the city limits. I had a great job, my son was doing great in school and I was about to purchase a house. My life was on the right track.

A few weeks went by and I had no communication from Marcus. Eventually, he called and asked if he could visit. The weather on this particular night was stormy and consisted of torrential rain and thunderstorms. In spite of this, I said, "Yes." I had bought a gift for his baby and wanted to give it to him. Although Alexis and I had arguments on the telephone, I did not have a problem with purchasing a gift for their child. The child had nothing to do with the fact that she had two crazy ass parents. Besides, Alexis was broke, with no job and crazy. Marcus was just disgraceful.

Marcus arrived around eight, looking suave and handsome as ever, but I wasn't going to be fooled this time. I was clear about our relationship status. He was my child's father and that was the extent of the relationship. I declined to be a part of his web of confusion any longer. Their baby was three weeks old. As far as I was concerned, it was time for me to move on. Up to that point, Marcus had only attended one doctor's appointment with me. He had not purchased anything for my baby and he simply showed no interested in participating in my pregnancy.

Yet still, I was glad to see him. We chatted for a while, catching up on what was happening in each other's lives. He talked about how happy he was to have a little girl. He didn't mention anything about Alexis. He also didn't mention anything about us reuniting, despite the big performance he put on three weeks earlier.

It was a school night and Dionte' was sound asleep. As Marcus was about to leave, the door bell rang. Jokingly I said, "That's your crazy baby mama." Marcus opened the door. There was Alexis, holding a silver, aluminum bat, with the look of Satan in her eyes.

Alexis was soaking wet from the rain. The long tracks in her hair were matted on her head. The intensity of hatred in her eyes gave her the most evil look I had ever seen. If looks could kill, I would have dissipated into thin air. At that very moment, she instantly reminded me of Freddie Kruger from Nightmare on Elm Street.

She was evil and her mission was to steal, kill, and destroy anything that was happening in that townhouse. The pouring rain and the lighting flashing behind her, as she held the bat was a scene I could not have imagined. Now I know how all the victims in the scary movies felt.

She started screaming at the top of her lungs, "It's after 10:00!" In my mind, I was wondering... *What the hell does that mean?* She swung the bat and hit Marcus across the shoulder. As she looked at me and headed my way, it was obvious I was her target. The force of the aluminum bat knocked him off balance causing him to stagger, but not to fall. I was standing behind Marcus on the stairs, but immediately moved out of the way into the kitchen.

This was my first time seeing Alexis Mason in person. As our eyes met, I was astonished this was the girl Marcus was choosing over me. I didn't see anything pretty, just a whole lot of ugly. As they say, beauty is in the eyes of the beholder. Marcus must have been absolutely blind.

Maybe it was the rain that made her look like a wild maniac, but I didn't see anything impressive about this girl. She had on a grey sweat suit and worn out Timberland boots. She looked about five feet eight, which made her like a giant "he-woman". Her skin was dark and ashy. She had the darkest eyes and the biggest lips I'd seen on a woman. Maybe that's what hooked Marcus.

When I came to my senses, Alexis was screaming, "Bitch, I'm going to kick that baby out of your stomach!" and coming after me with the bat. Marcus jumped in front of me, grabbed the bat, and pushed her against the wall. I fell against the kitchen sink.

As Marcus was attempting to hold Alexis back, she managed to extend her leg around him and kick me repeatedly in the stomach, with her dusty Timberland boots. The small kitchen didn't leave much room for getting out of the way, but I had to find something to defend myself against this lunatic.

Like a mad woman, I picked up a chair and started swinging. Fortunately for her, Marcus pushed her out of the house. I slammed the door behind him and locked it.

I was furious that I could not get back at that insane bitch. The only thing that kept me from going after her was the fact that I was six months pregnant. I wanted to rip the weave out of her head and beat the shit out of her, but I had to be sensible and think about my baby.

Who the fuck did she think she was dealing with? Kicking a pregnant woman. Who does that? Who tries to fight a pregnant, defenseless woman? Now that her baby was born, I was fair game to her. She could attack me at anytime and I could not adequately defend myself.

I didn't know what to do. I didn't have a gun. Otherwise, I would have blown her brains away. She came into my house and violated the code. Even in the hood, people know you don't fight a pregnant woman. All that I worked for to change my life and become a respectable teacher had gone out of the window.

I promised as soon as I had this baby, I was going to fuck Alexis up. The beating was going to be brutal to a point of no return. The anger was getting the best of me. I peered through the window and couldn't believe my eyes. Marcus was actually trying to explain to that bitch why he was at my house.

"Alexis, look! Look at this." Marcus was holding up the gift bag I bought. "She bought you a gift for the baby. That's the only reason I'm here."

Alexis was still trying to get pass him to get to the door. "Alexis stop!" Marcus was begging more than commanding. "There is nothing going on between us. Why are you acting like this?"

I couldn't tell if he was referring to us or them. The saddest part was watching him wave the gift I had bought them in her face, justifying his whereabouts.

"You are mine! I already told you that! We are a family. Since you won't leave her alone, I'm going to kill her. Is that what you want, Marcus? Is that the only way to get rid of her? You think she is all that, so I'm going to take care of it, Marcus. You WILL leave her alone and you WILL be my man. Do you understand me Marcus?" Marcus was looking real crazy at this point.

Then she started yelling, "That's okay, bitch! I'm coming back with a gun and I'm going to shoot ya ass." She turned to Marcus and said, "You better leave. I'm going to murder that bitch, tonight!"

I was in complete shock. I could not believe that bitch came into my house, tried to beat me with a bat, and kill my unborn child. Furthermore, Marcus, the man of my dreams was trying to calm *her* down and explain the situation to *her*. Was this really the life I wanted with Marcus?

After she sped off in her car, I opened the door for Marcus. He kept saying, "Are you okay? I am so sorry." He didn't know I saw him through the window begging Alexis to stop, but I didn't mention it. He sat the torn, soggy gift bag on the table.

The cramps in my stomach made it difficult for me to walk. The kicks obviously shook up the baby. I was afraid that some serious damage was done to the baby, but I wanted to inform the police of Alexis' threats, just in case she actually came back with a gun. Instead of calling the police, Marcus and I went to the police station. We dragged Dionte' along in the cold, wet rain. Luckily, he was still asleep and didn't hear the commotion.

Marcus filed the police report. It was so vague that you would think the incident was not a big deal. It read….

September 25, 2000

The above defendant rang the doorbell to which I opened the door because I was leaving. The defendant then struck me in the shoulder and proceeded to kick Miss Jones in the stomach. I then physically removed the defendant and she told me that I should leave because she would be back with a gun. LaKeacha Jones is a friend. Alexis Mason is the mother of my daughter. She used an aluminum bat to hit me in the shoulder. Another police report was filed at Woodlawn Precinct for an incident that occurred in the fall of 1999 pertaining to Alexis Mason. My shoulder is sore. It hurts when I move my arm around.

After leaving the police station, we hurried to the emergency room to check on the baby. The baby was okay, but the doctors required me to stay overnight to make sure she continued breathing.

The next morning, I left the hospital feeling drained and confused. Marcus took Dionte' to school and dropped me off at my house, as if nothing happened. Maybe he was use to this type of drama with Alexis, but this was unacceptable. I laid down to take a brief nap.

The ringing of the telephone startled me. Without checking the caller ID, I answered, "Hello."

"Keacha, don't hang up." It was Alexis, so I listened.

"Are you and the baby okay? I'm a mother and I know how it is. I came over there to bash Marcus' car in, then I saw red and rung the doorbell. Whatever consequences I have to suffer, I will."

Yeah, Bitch you will suffer. I didn't respond and hung up the telephone. I was convinced that this bitch was psychotic. *How the fuck you gonna come to my house, try to kill my baby and then call me the next morning and apologize like nothing happened. Is this shit for real? I must be in a twilight zone.*

I called my mother to tell her what was happening. She asked for Alexis' number and called her. Alexis apologized to my mother and said she wouldn't bother me again. I decided to go to the police station to file my own complaint. I didn't feel comfortable with Marcus' complaint, because he would probably drop the charges against her. He never told me about an incident that occurred the previous year between them. Obviously, he didn't take the matter any further, because she was still pursuing him. For some reason, he seemed to be protecting her. *LaKeacha Jones is a friend. Alexis Mason is the mother of my daughter.* That statement stuck with me for a long time.

My complaint read……

September 26, 2000

The above defendant rang my doorbell at approximately 10:00 p.m. My friend, her ex-boyfriend, opened the door as he was leaving. Ms. Mason was standing at my door. She started yelling and hit him with the bat. She tried to push him out of the way while swinging the bat continuously at me. Although the bat did not hit me, Ms. Mason was close enough to kick me in my stomach continuously, while still attempting to hit me with the bat. I am six months pregnant and Ms. Mason is aware of this. I proceeded to fall against the kitchen sink while Marcus pushed Ms. Mason out of the door. I proceeded to lock the door and contacted the police. Because of the severe kicking I received to the stomach, I stayed overnight in the emergency room to make sure my baby was alive. Ms. Mason was completely aware I was pregnant and almost killed my unborn child. Ms. Mason also contacted my home several times last night and this morning. Ms. Mason called my house previously on numerous occasions came to my home uninvited and threatened to come back with a gun to kill me. Because I am six months pregnant, I have no way of defending myself against Ms. Mason. My life and the safety of my children are at risk.

The police officers said a warrant would be issued for Alexis' arrest. *Great!* I thought. *Get that psychotic bitch off the streets until I have my baby.* After filing my police report, I called Tracy to tell her about the incident. She went ballistic.

"Where the fuck does that bitch live? I'm going to fuck her up. Let me call Shawna and Anecia."

"Calm down, calm down," I said.

"I'm good. I want this bitch for myself. Just wait until I have this baby. She thinks she's playing with a lil girl, but I'm going to beat her ass like a grown woman."

After that incident, I began to speed up my search for a new home. Alexis would probably try something else to get rid of my baby, so I needed to move quickly. The house in Chase was too far from my family and friends. If anything else went down, at least I would be closer to getting the help I needed. I couldn't depend on Marcus to protect me, but I knew my family and friends would be there no matter what.

It didn't take long for me to find a house in a nice neighborhood. The house was in Northeast Baltimore. It was a single family, three bedroom house with a full basement. The master bedroom was fit for a queen. It covered the entire upstairs. I really loved the huge backyard that opened to an enormous park. I visualized myself playing with my children in the wonderful park and having the biggest crab feasts in my backyard.

Most of my neighbors were Caucasian, except for two African American families; one lived across the street with a lot of boys and another lady and her son, lived a little further up the street. Yep, I did it again. I accomplished another goal. At the age of 25, I was a home owner.

I went to settlement on October 13 and moved in the house the next day. Marcus moved all of my furniture himself. This was one reason I was in love with him. He packed, unpacked and set up all of the furniture in the house. He didn't try to move in, though. He came to visit more often, but never stayed overnight.

I was anxious to set up the baby's room. Instead of the usual pink, I decorated the baby's room in a pretty mint green, with pastel colored balloons. The furniture was a beautiful light oak wood. It was perfect for my pretty little princess, in my pretty little house.

Marcus and I began talking more. He felt comfortable coming over, now that Alexis did not know where I lived. I still wasn't sure where the relationship was going. I didn't know if we were together or not.

One Saturday, Marcus brought his daughter over. Unfortunately, she was the spitting image of her mother. She kept crying this screeching cry. I thought maybe something was wrong with her, since her mother had taken those pills in attempt to get rid of her. Alexis sent the baby out of the house with a dirty car seat and a filthy diaper bag. Marcus said she didn't want him to get the good stuff. *The good stuff. How much sense does that make? You have a pile full of dirty stuff designated for sending your baby out the house with.* I thought. *Marcus has got himself a true looney.*

After Marcus took the baby home, he spent the night at my house for the first time. The next morning, his car was severely scratched. The scratch went from the front headlight to the brake light on the passenger side of his car. Alexis must have gotten someone to follow him. Marcus noted that Alexis kept stalling and pushing up on him, when he dropped off the baby. Marcus left my house and went to Alexis' house to find out why she scratched his car. Of course, she denied it. Coincidentally, he saw an ice pick on her counter.

The following Saturday morning, November 11, the telephone rang very early. When I answered, there was silence, but I could hear heavy breathing. I hung up the phone. They called back repeatedly. I knew it was Alexis. *How did she get my number again?* Later that afternoon, Tracy and her boyfriend, Norman, came to visit. The phone continued to ring non-stop.

Tracy answered the telephone and said, "Alexis, why the fuck do you keep calling here? I already owe you an ass whooping. You're lucky I don't know where you live, you lil stupid bitch! If I ever find you on the streets, rock a bye bitch!" Tracy hung up the phone. The phone rang again. This time Norman answered.

"Hello?"

"May I speak to Keacha?" a man asked.

"Naw, this is her boyfriend. Who is this?" said Norman.

"You ain't her boyfriend, nigga. Tell that bitch she better watch her back. I'm the Clean Up Man."

Norman said, "Listen partner, you tell that bitch, Alexis, she better watch her back, Clean Up Man. Nigga, game time is over. I have stepped into the picture and y'all don't want to deal with me, partner. All this lil tit for tat is gonna end, immediately. Kicking my girl while she is pregnant is a bull shit move; and your punk ass sitting there encouraging a bitch to fight a pregnant women. Nigga, you ain't shit! It's a time and place for everything my man, and y'all time is up. I tell you what, Mr. Clean Up Man, y'all know the address, so come on over. Let's end this bullshit right here and right now. Cause I promise you, you will never see the light of day again."

The line went dead.

Norman and Tracy had been together for a while. Like most guys we dealt with, Norman was a thug. He was on the path of getting his life together, but he was definitely from the streets. He knew how to get things done and he was about his business. He was puzzled at how Marcus let things get this far, but nevertheless, he was determined to fix it. As far as we were concerned, they were just bullshitting, trying to scare me. Nevertheless,

Marcus and Tracy stayed over, waiting for something to pop off. All was quiet.

As a matter of fact, the next few days were extremely calm. I was surprised that Alexis didn't call the house her normal thirty times a day, nor did my cell phone ring with any strange numbers. *Maybe Norman scared her or maybe it finally clicked that she needed to move on with her life.*

What a beautiful day. I thought as I started cleaning up my classroom. *The kids were great in class today and Marcus brought my favorite lunch; a crab cake with potato salad and a large half & half.* My due date was December 18, only a month away. I wanted to be prepared so I wrote six weeks' worth of lesson plans, in case the baby came early. I made all of my students' notebooks, with enough homework for six weeks.

Dionte' and his father were establishing a great relationship, so he picked Dionte' up from school at least once a week. Today he was keeping him until 6:00 that evening. I was able to stay at work a little later than usual and get some things prepared.

As I was leaving work, I received a private call on my cell phone. I brushed it off and thought. *Not again. How did this crazy bitch get my cell phone number? This is becoming ridiculous. She does not know when to quit.* I had an eerie feeling, but ignored it.

I drove home and began cleaning up. Marcus usually came over on Thursdays, but he didn't mention coming over tonight, when he brought my lunch. As we were talking on the phone, I heard a noise outside of the kitchen window. I was so engaged in my conversation with Marcus, I disregarded it.

Marcus and I were laughing and joking, making light of the conversation with the "Clean Up Man" on Saturday.

"You know what Marcus; I think Alexis wrote that song that Jennifer Holiday sings."

"What song?"Marcus asked laughing.

"And I am telling you! I'm not going. You're the best man I'll ever know. There's no way I can ever go. No, No, there's no way. NO! NO! NO! NOOOOO way, I'm living without you." I started singing the song in the best Jennifer Holliday rendition I could. We both broke out into laughter. The door bell rung.

"Hold on. That's Maurice, six o' clock on the dot." I told Marcus and sat the phone on the counter in the kitchen."

CHAPTER 4: DANGER ZONE

"Into each life, some rain must fall; some days must be dark and dreary."
Henry Wadsworth Longfellow

I turned on the porch light and looked through the glass window above the door. It wasn't Maurice ringing the doorbell.

"Excuse me." The man said. "I live across the street, and your mail came to our house." He held up an envelope.

As I was attempting to open the door, the top lock jammed and wouldn't open. I looked out of the window again and hesitated, *"This is odd. Why would he wait so late to bring me mail. Let me get a good look at this man."* I contemplated telling him to put the mail in the mailbox, but I didn't want to seem impolite to my new neighbors. *If anything happens, he's brown skin, medium height, has a long face with an extremely large nose and lips.*

I was still struggling to unlock the top lock on the door. As soon as the door unlocked, he forcefully pushed it saying, "Is Dante here? Is Dante here?" I stumbled back as he pushed passed me, as if he were searching for somebody or something.

In hindsight, I should've paid attention to the signs showing me to keep the door closed. The creepy feeling I had, warned me that something wasn't right, but I ignored it. *What the hell is he doing? Is he looking for Dionte'? Is this man high? Maybe he is in the wrong house. I need to get some help.*

It still didn't dawn on me that this may have been the "Clean Up Man" and Alexis was behind this set up. Thinking he would pull me inside the house, I darted towards the stairs of the front porch. He didn't come after me at all. I had escaped. I was saved.

Just then, two people dressed in black, came from the side of the steps, behind the bushes, startling me. I didn't know which way to turn. The man was in the house, so I couldn't run back inside the house and two other people were in front of me, blocking my escape. I slid backwards and fell on the steps.

I started screaming, "Marcus!" remembering that he was still on the phone on the kitchen table. I didn't know if he could hear me, but I shouted anyway as loud as I could. If Marcus heard me, he would know that something was wrong and call the police. It's six in the evening, but its pitch black outside. No one is outside, walking or driving. I'm all alone, trapped.

"Stop, I'm pregnant!" I shrieked. The assailants showed no mercy. It took a moment for me to realize their mission was to intentionally kill my unborn daughter. Fighting back was useless. I curled myself into a ball and held onto the stair rail, trying to protect my stomach and my face. The stomps were grueling and deliberate. The ridges of the Timberland boots tread heavily in my head, on my face, in my back, but trying most intentionally to get to my stomach. The blows to my head caused me to feel lightheaded. Whenever they weren't kicking; they were punching me, with all of their might.

Look at a face. Get a glimpse. I was trying to look at a face, but every time I looked up. "Bam!" I was kicked in the face. I was able to sneak a quick look at the one attacker who wore a black mask under a black sweatshirt, fully covered. I could see breast imprints, but I couldn't see a face. Her kicks exerted extra force and were unbelievably gruesome. It was personal with her.

The other aggressor was a light skinned girl, with a round face. She wore a black knit hat, only covering some of her sandy brown hair. Her face was not covered, but I didn't recognize her, although she resembled the girl with the baby. Her hits and kicks were less compelling. She stayed at the bottom of the stairs, close to the sidewalk, as if she were scared.

I felt weaker and weaker, but I continued holding on tightly to the stair rail, trying my best to cover my stomach. The odds were against me and I feared for my life. My thoughts were all over the place. *I can't believe this bitch sneak attacked me. I'm going to fuck her up. What the hell is that man doing in my house? I hope he is not destroying my new table set my mother bought me.*

The guy came out of the house and said "Take out the shit and burn that bitch alive."

"Somebody help me! Help Me!" I yelled.

The beating stopped momentarily. The neighborhood was silent. Still no one was in sight. I didn't know if anyone would come out to help a neighbor who just moved in a month ago.

I'm about to die! Oh God, they're going to shoot me in the head. The Lord is my Sheppard. I shall not want. I started praying. The girl covered in black, grabbed a small bottle out of her pocket and poured liquid directly in my head and on my face. She held my face with one hand and continued pouring until the container was empty.

"Aghhhhh!" I struggled to protect my stomach now. I was desperately trying to close my eyes and mouth, while holding on to the rail. The acid was burning my skin on contact.

"Aghhhhh!" I continued to scream, hoping someone would come to my rescue. *I'm burning! I'm on fire! Oh, my God!* The chemicals were in my eyes. I couldn't see. It was in my mouth. I was trying to scream, *HELP ME!* But the chemicals were burning my tongue and eating through my skin. The girl in all black attempted to cover my mouth to stop me from screaming. I bit her hand. *Bitch, take that.* Then I realized that she had on black gloves, causing her to be fully covered in black, except for those dirty Timberland boots, I noticed on the steps.

I cringed in agony and couldn't protect my unborn baby anymore. I was in tremendous pain. It was three against one, and they were all kicking and stomping me. I remained curled up on the steps, recognizing that if I let go of that rail, they would have full access to my stomach and would beat me until my baby and I were dead. I caught a glimpse of the light skinned girl running away, leaving the guy and the other girl in black still kicking me.

"Help Me, Somebody, Please!" I felt weaker with every kick. I knew my baby was dead. I was losing consciousness and acknowledged that Alexis Mason had finally won. She was a woman scorned and had a score to settle. I was the target of her fury and rage. The anger she exhibited was deep and profound. Unlike her friend who ran off, Alexis would not stop until she had beaten the life out of my baby and destroyed my face beyond recognition. With this knowledge, I stopped screaming and whispered, "Jesus".

Instantly, a calm feeling came over me. I prayed, *"God please protect my baby."* I wasn't screaming anymore. I felt myself going faint, but I mustered enough energy to say, "Alexis, you need to stop. I know it's you and I'm going to fuck you up." I was down, but I was not defeated. I still wanted her to know that no matter how much black she wore, I knew it was her. My statement startled her. She paused, as if she were shocked that I identified her.

I heard people coming to my rescue. "Call the police! Get my gun!" someone exclaimed. My heart was beating sporadically. A million thoughts were racing through my head: *Am I dying? I can't lose my daughter. God, I'm not ready to die. It's so quiet. I felt peaceful. I'm going to live. November 16, 2000 is not my resting date.*

All of a sudden, Bam! Another kick in the head, snapped me out of my thoughts. The kick had so much force that my neck snapped out of place from the impact. Even though my vision was blurry, and the chemicals consumed my eyes, I peeped up to see the last two assailants running away. *They're gone. It's over. Mission accomplished. They've killed my baby.*

Every part of my body was in pain. The chemicals continued to burn rapidly through my skin. My neighbors, the lady and her young son came over to rescue me. Other neighbors approached the house while, calling 911. The little boy went and found some shoes for me. I had only been in the house for a month and had not met any of my neighbors. I didn't know these people, but they saved my life.

I sat there crying, beaten in every way possible. I was furious that I could not defend myself against Alexis. I was stupid to take her threats as jokes. I brushed her off and didn't think she would plan an attack like this.

The police and ambulance arrived. The paramedics were trying to subdue the chemicals, but it was burning fast. The paramedics cut off my shirt, but my bra held much of the chemicals so my breasts continued burning.

I was screaming for Marcus and hoping my son didn't pull up and see all of this commotion. I was going in and out of consciousness, but all I could think about was killing Alexis, getting revenge. Even in agony, I promised I was going to kill her straight up.

The police officer began asking me questions. "Do you know who did this?"

"Alexis. Alexis Mason." Then I went unconscious.

The more I thought about plotting revenge, the harder it was for me to breath. I could hear the paramedics saying, "She's not breathing. Her baby is dying."

At that point, I could hear, but I couldn't speak. I was praying to God to get me out of this. In all the years I grew up in church, I never prayed the way I was praying now. Cussing in one minute and praying, the next minute. Then something strange happened.

An overwhelming sadness came over me as I thought about the little girl that I was supposed to bring in this world. Her life would be taken by an evil, monstrous female whose jealously and rage pushed her to the limits of killing an unborn child. My daughter was an innocent bystander of a love triangle gone terribly wrong. There was no justification for her being prematurely buried before she had a chance to live. At that moment, I promised God that I would not kill Alexis if he spared my baby's life.

The ambulance rushed me to the Johns Hopkins Hospital Burn Unit. I became conscious and started screaming for Marcus. The nurses told me to calm down and they would get him. They immediately cut off the remaining clothes and began scraping my skin. Afterwards they placed me, completely naked, in a wheelchair, covered with only a blanket and rushed me down the halls.

The nurses removed the blanket and pushed me into an enormous industrial walk-in shower. The chilly water blasted out like a fire extinguisher, as I sat in the wheelchair, unable to move. The excruciating pain from the burns mixed with the robust force of the water, insulted my injuries even more. Big clumps of hair fell into my lap as I held my head down, trying to avoid the pressure of the water gushing directly in my face.

The nurses lingered in the corner laughing because water was splashing on them and they didn't want to get wet. *Bitches. I'm burning. My skin and hair are falling out and y'all worried about getting wet.* The anger, the fear, and the hatred caused me to cry non-stop. The tears dissolved with the water. *There is no need of crying. You need to be strong for your little girl. You can beat this.* With tears still flowing, I stayed under the pressure of the freezing water for at least thirty minutes, still astonished by what had occurred that evening.

At last, I was dressed with a hospital gown and taken to a room. The room had no mirrors on the wall, so I could not see the damage that had been done. Marcus scurried into the room. Distress and anguish were all over his face. I burst into tears again. He held me tightly, but my body ached in pain.

"Shh," Marcus whispered. "I'm going to handle this."

"Where's Dionte'?" I asked. "Don't let him see me like this."

"He is still with his dad. Maurice and I drove up at the same time. The ambulance had just pulled off. Dionte' was in the car. He doesn't know what happened. Maurice will take him to school in the morning."

A few minutes later, Angie, Tracy, my mother and Aunt Izzy rushed into the room.

"Oh, my God!" my sister yelled.

My mother looked like she wanted to cry, but she remained calm. I could see the hurt and pain in my aunt's face. She came and held my hand, which caused the tears to start again. They were trying to be strong for me. From the looks on their faces, I could tell, I was fucked up pretty bad.

An older white doctor came into the room. He had a very calm spirit. "LaKeacha, seems like you had a rough night."

"Yeah."

"We are running test to see what chemicals were in the substance thrown on you." I was worried about my baby more than myself. The doctor noticed the distressing look in my eyes and said, "The obstetrician is coming in to check the baby. Do you know what you are having?"

"I'm having a girl."

"She's a strong little girl, like her mama," the doctor smiled. At that moment, I wasn't strong. I was at the weakest point of my life. I was defeated. Just then the obstetrician walked in with his equipment. He placed the stethoscope on my stomach. He looked confused as he placed the stethoscope in different places on my stomach.

"I can't hear a heartbeat," the doctor stated. "I need a sonogram."

My heart felt as if someone sucked all of the life out of me. My ears went deaf. I was in a dark place in my mind. No one could save me now. It was nothing anyone in that room could do to save my baby. It was between me and God. I needed him, more than I had ever needed him before.

Before today, I couldn't remember the last time I prayed. I couldn't remember if I ever prayed. Of course, I taught my son, the Our Father's Prayer and the Daily Grace, but other than that, I had no communication with God.

Since the church, made me apologize for getting pregnant and treated me so badly, I perceived God to be mean and unforgiving. At this point, I needed someone stronger and more powerful than the doctors. God was the only one who could help me. *If I could convince him to listen to me, maybe he will help me.*

So I prayed some more. *Lord, I promised you that I would change, if you spared my daughter's life. Please God. I know I'm not perfect, but I didn't deserve this. I'm sorry for getting pregnant. I'm sorry for not going to church. I'm sorry for messing up Antoine's car. I'm sorry for going off on Alexis.* I was trying to think of all the things I needed to apologize for, so God could spare my baby's life. To me, these things were minor. Nevertheless, I needed God to help me.

Moments later, the sonographer came in to do the ultrasound. She placed the device on my stomach and moved it in different places, just as the doctor had done. We didn't hear a heartbeat. Then she used the vaginal ultrasound to check my uterus.

"There she is!" the sonographer said excitingly.

"She's hiding, but she's alive. Let me see if I can move her around so you can hear the heartbeat."

This time, when she placed the sonogram on my stomach we could hear the heartbeat. The heartbeat brought some joy to this miserable night of Thursday, November 16, 2000; the night I will never forget.

Out of all that was happening I had several things to be fortunate about: my baby girl was alive, my son wasn't home to witness this tragedy, Marcus was on the phone to alert the police and I wasn't pushed inside of the house, where I would never have gotten out alive. Lastly, I was grateful the three assailants were punk ass bitches, who didn't have any balls, because real niggas would have killed me. Despite, my conflicting spirit, I knew there was a God and he wasn't so mean after all. He spared my child's life.

The doctors sent me to another room to stay overnight. Marcus and Tracy covered all of the mirrors. When everybody left, I got up to use the bathroom. *I must be hideous the way they are covering these mirrors.* I tore down the paper, covering one of the mirrors.

"Aghhhhhhhh!" a shriek that sounded like death ranged through the hospital. Hideous, unsightly, dreadful are the words to describe what I saw. Monstrous. My skin went from caramel brown to charcoal black. The parts that were still brown had black spots all over them. My face was three times its normal size. My blood shot red eyes bulged from my head. My once small lips were now enormous and twisted. Nasty cuts covered my neck and upper part of my body. Small patches of hair remained on the scalp of my head, which was otherwise bald. My chest was covered with black scaly skin. Fluid and blood were leaking from my breast.

Nurses and doctors rushed to the bathroom. I was screaming and crying hysterically. I couldn't believe I would look like a monster for the rest of my life. Not that I was Halle Berry before, but now I looked worse than Alexis. As a matter fact, I looked like the elephant man, the movie where the man was so ugly that he wore a bag over his head. Alexis succeeded at making me look hideous. *How would my son handle my horrible face? How was I going to stand before my students looking like a dreadful monster? Surely, Marcus would leave me now.*

The nurses managed to get me back in the bed. I put the covers over my head, crying underneath. "Keacha." I heard a soft spoken voice. "Keacha, take the covers off of your head." Pastor Williams came back to the hospital with my mother that night and prayed for me. As much as I had distanced myself from God and the church, they still loved me. Pastor Williams' soft words and prayers caused me to sleep peacefully that night. I needed the rest. This was the beginning of a long, drawn out battle. A battle never imagined.

CHAPTER 5:
TO PROTECT AND TO SERVE

"Good people do not need laws to tell them to act responsibly, while bad people will find a way around the laws."

Plato

Baltimore City Police detectives arrived at the hospital, that Saturday, two days after the incident. Detective Vaughn and Detective Shaw seemed very preoccupied as I told them what happened. Detective Vaughn was a tall light-skinned man, who was proud of the fact he was a shooting detective, because he kept mentioning it. He was presumably the bad cop.

Detective Shaw was a shorter, heavy weight, dark-skinned detective. He seemed more interested in the case than Detective Vaughn. After getting all of the details of that horrific evening, Detective Vaughn asked, "How do you know Alexis Mason did this to you, if you couldn't see her face?

I started thinking. *I didn't have any enemies except for Alexis. Who else would intentionally try to kill my baby? She told several people that I should not have been pregnant and she was going to kick that baby out of my stomach. Who else would want my face messed up so bad to pour chemicals directly onto it? Who else would break in a house, but not steal anything? Who else knew that I would fall for the envelope trick, like I fell for the telephone trick with her friend? Why would the other two culprits leave their face open, except the one person with the black face mask and knit gloves?* It wasn't enough that Alexis had threatened me a few days earlier and I had charges against her for kicking me in my stomach. So I lied.

"I heard the guy call her name."

If I had known that still wasn't enough, I would have said, I saw her face. Nevertheless, I was confident the detectives would at least question Alexis about her whereabouts that night. After I described the other two assailants, the detectives assured me they would follow up and bring some mug shots for me to identify the man who rung the doorbell.

After staying in the hospital for three days, it was confirmed I had first, second and third degree burns on my head, face and chest. The chemicals thrown on me were made up of bleach, lye and sulfuric acid. I suffered extensive tissue damage and would need surgery to repair the damaged caused to the tissue in my breast. To treat the other areas, I would applying dressing to the burns each day and return to the burn clinic at least once a week. I was released to go home on Sunday.

Coming home proved to be more difficult than I expected and brought back bad memories of that evening. The stained stairs and fingerprint dust on my door reminded me of the incident and I collapsed. Reliving the incident, over and over again in my head, caused me to be emotionally drained and paranoid. Marcus put me in the bed and went outside to clean the steps. As he was cleaning the steps, he spotted a black knitted glove and put it in some plastic.

My family arrived to the house later that evening to discuss how to get revenge on Alexis. My cousins were true Baltimore City thugs, not to be disrespected or provoked. The situation would not be handled lightly. Convincing them to spare Alexis' life was going to be difficult. Keeping my promise to God was going to be even more challenging.

"This bitch is crazy as shit. We need to kill her ass," my cousin, Shane said. "Fucking her up ain't going to do shit. She will continue to go back and forth. Let's put this bitch in the grave, tonight!"

"No! I'm okay. I don't want y'all to get in trouble." I said. I didn't want anybody going to jail or getting hurt on my account. Besides, I promised God that I would not kill her.

"Don't you worry about that," said Big Boy. My cousin Big Boy was younger than me, but he was about three hundred pounds and six feet. He often served as a bouncer at many of the nightclubs. Although he was sweet as he could be under normal circumstances, at this moment he was hot as a firecracker. "Ain't nobody getting in trouble. I'm going to blow the whole fuckin' house up. It won't be a drop of evidence I was there." Big Boy turns to Marcus, "Yo, what's Alexis address? Tell her to get your kid out of the house. Is that aight with you?"

"Man, I don't care what y'all do." stated Marcus.

Big Boy jumped across the room and started choking Marcus. Shane, his little brother stopped him, but then turned his fury towards Marcus.

"Man, how you gonna let your own child get blown up? You ain't shit. You allowed this shit to happen to my cousin. Your punk ass should have handled this." Shane yelled. Shane was also younger than me, but was definitely known for popping a nigga in a heartbeat. I was surprised he held Big Boy back.

My cousins were furious with Marcus. They couldn't believe he allowed this to happen. Cool was even angrier because he tried to warn Marcus about Alexis. Cool was nicknamed that for a reason, normally, he would be the sane one, thinking rationally, but now Cool was mad as hell and that meant trouble. The house was in a complete uproar now. Everybody started saying what they would do, but nobody really knows what they will do until it happens to them.

Aunt Gertrude said, "Keacha, why would you open the door in the first place? You didn't know the guy, so that didn't make sense to open the door."

With tears in my eyes, I stated. "Every day since Thursday, I wished I didn't open that damn door. So it's my fault I got beat up and burned for opening my damn door. If I didn't open the door, they would have gotten me anyway. They were trying to get inside the house. Can you imagine how many hours they could have beaten me if they had gotten into the house? Do you know how horrific it would have been if my son were here? So I'm glad it happened like that because it could have been worse."

I was very hurt and angry Aunt Gertrude would blame me for this incident. It never occurred to me that Alexis would take things this far. I had conflicts with females before, but it was never like this. I assumed she would eventually get tired of the games, stop calling me and go on with her life.

However, I had never dealt with a psychotic female like Alexis Mason before. Her fixation became with me, not Marcus, like most females. She thought if she could mess me up, then Marcus would not want to be with me anymore. She wanted to break me and her mission was being accomplished. My family was arguing about what to do next. Marcus was distressed. I had no peace in my home. My life was chaotic, thanks to Alexis Mason. Instead of staying at my house, I packed a bag and went to my mother's apartment throughout the week. On the weekends, I came home with Marcus. To protect the baby, I was never alone.

Monday morning, Marcus called me. "I can't believe this bitch just called me screaming about not coming to pick up the baby on Saturday."

"Are you serious? What did she say?" I asked.

"She didn't care what was going on in my life, her baby came first and she wanted to let me know the police were looking for her. She had to turn herself in for the warrant *you* wrote for the bat incident."

"What did you say to her?"

"I didn't respond to her. The new warrant is what triggered the whole retaliation on Thursday. Keacha, I wanna kill that bitch so bad."

"No, Marcus. That's what she wants. You would be ruining your life."

"I know this is my entire fault and your family is furious with me. I'm trying to figure out how to fix everything."

"Hold on, Marcus. Someone is on the other line."

"Hello, may I speak to LaKeacha Jones?"

"Who's calling?"

"I am calling from Financial Aid Services."

I disconnected the line and clicked back to Marcus. "You won't believe this. That was a guy pretending to be someone from financial aid calling for me. Financial aid has never called me before, especially at my mother's house, why would they call now?"

"How did she get your mother's number?"

"The morning after she kicked me, my mother called her. Of course, my mother didn't know how to block her number. I need to call the detectives. Now she is stalking me. This is harassment. I hope she doesn't have my mother's address."

Night terrors had taken over my sleep each night. I felt like someone was choking the life out of me. Screaming, kicking and crying in my sleep, was the nightly torture. I woke up breathless, trembling and shaking. My sheets were soaked in sweat and tears. My mother rushed into my room and prayed for me. Gradually, my breathing returned to normal and I slept, praying for a peaceful rest.

My aunts thought Alexis put voodoo on me because it was rumored all kinds of voodoo flourished in her family. Out of concern, they went to a voodoo priestess in South Carolina to bind Alexis from hurting me. Again, they asked me if I wanted her dead. "No. I want her to leave me alone." I said, holding steadfast to my promise to God.

My aunt instructed the voodoo priestess to stop Alexis from hurting me again, but not kill her, per my request. I was told to keep a picture of Alexis (that I stole from Marcus) in a jar of black solution the voodoo priestess concocted. I kept the jar in a dark space in the back of the closet. In addition, I had to wear a piece of cloth in my shoe for protection to keep Alexis from coming near me again, especially while I was pregnant.

I was still desperate to get some solutions to dealing with Alexis while I was pregnant. Ms. Emma and Tracy suggested I visit Prophet

Herman. He would look into the future and tell me some things I needed to know about the situation. Tracy and I went to a senior citizens home to see Prophet Herman. Prophet Herman was a fat man with tons of gold necklaces around his neck and a gold ring on each finger.

He looked at me and said, "What's going on with you? I sense a lot of sadness." I told him about Alexis.

"This girl is mentally ill. You need protection from her. Read Psalms 91 and 27 every day, while looking towards the east. Get yourself a Star of David and wear it for protection. You also need an alert that you can carry to call the police on contact. This girl is obsessed with you and she will try to attack you again."

"I see some people coming through a basement window. Get a registered gun and protect yourself at all times. This baby is a girl. She will be very anointed and will love to sing. Keep her under an anointed preacher. You will be moving to another state. I cannot figure out this man, Marcus. He does not love her, but he likes the sexual favors she does for him. Don't worry yourself. I will bind her up, so you will be safe." Then, he did some rituals to bind Alexis from hurting me again.

I never told Prophet Herman I was having a girl, so it was confirmation he was a true prophet. I did everything he told me. I scheduled an alarm system to be installed in my house. I read Psalm 91 and Psalm 27 everyday, facing towards the East. I wore my Star of David around my neck for protection and I got a .357 magnum.

Psalm 91 reads…
Whoever dwells in the shelter of the Most High, will rest in the shadow of the Almighty. I will say of the LORD, "He is my refuge and my fortress, my God, in whom I trust." Surely he will save you from the fowler's snare and from the deadly pestilence. He will cover you with his feathers, and under his wings you will find refuge; his faithfulness will be your shield and rampart. You will not fear the terror of night, nor the arrow that flies by day, nor the pestilence that stalks in the darkness, nor the plague that destroys at midday. A thousand may fall at your side, ten thousand at your right hand, but it will not come near you. You will only observe with your eyes and see the punishment of the wicked. If you say, "The LORD is my refuge," and you make the Most High your dwelling, no harm will overtake you; no disaster will come near your tent. For he will command his angels concerning you to guard you in all your ways; they will lift you up in their hands, so that you will not strike your foot against a stone. You will tread on the lion and the cobra; you will trample the great lion and the serpent. "Because he loves me," says the LORD, "I will rescue him; I will protect him, for he acknowledges my name. He will call on me, and I will answer him; I will be with him in trouble, I will deliver him and honor him. With long life I will satisfy him and show him my salvation."

Psalm 27
The LORD is my light and my salvation, whom shall I fear?
The LORD is the stronghold of my life of whom shall I be afraid? When the wicked advance against me to devour me, it is my enemies and my foes who will stumble and fall. Though an army besiege me, my heart will not fear; though war break out against me, even then I will be confident. One thing I ask from the LORD, this only do I seek: that I may dwell in the house of the LORD, all the days of my life, to gaze on the beauty of the LORD and to seek him in his temple. For in the day of trouble, he will keep me safe in his dwelling; he will hide me in the shelter of his sacred tent and set me high upon a rock. Then my head will be exalted above the enemies who surround me; at his sacred tent I will sacrifice with shouts of joy; I will sing and make music to the LORD. Hear my voice when I call, LORD; be merciful to me and answer me. My heart says of you "Seek his face!"

Your face, LORD, I will seek. Do not hide your face from me, do not turn your servant away in anger; you have been my helper. Do not reject me or forsake me, God my Savior. Though my father and mother forsake me, the LORD will receive me. Teach me your way, LORD; lead me in a straight path because of my oppressors. Do not turn me over to the desire of my foes, for false witnesses rise up against me, spouting malicious accusations. I remain confident of this: I will see the goodness of the LORD in the land of the living. Wait for the LORD; be strong and take heart and wait for the LORD

Depending on Baltimore City Police Department to protect me, was useless. Every day I called Detective Vaughn to ask him if he picked up Alexis or if he had any information on the case. He would either be out of the office or say that he hadn't talked to her yet. He was unconcerned about the entire situation. He kept emphasizing he was a shooting detective and he didn't understand why he was put on this case.

I scheduled the installation for the security system on a Friday. As soon as I entered the house, the phone was ringing. Again, without looking at the caller ID, I answered the phone to Alexis, being belligerent.

"Bitch, what kind of games are you playing? Why is your stupid ass mother playing on my phone?" I hung up the phone. I had no idea what Alexis was referring to. My mother wasn't playing on her phone. She apparently was nervous because she didn't know where I was or what was going on. She called back again.

"Stop calling my fucking house! What the fuck do you want?" I yelled.

"Oh, you still got a lot of mouth. You, stupid bitch. That's why you got fucked up, running your mouth."

"Yeah, bitch, I got fucked up by you and your punk ass friends, hiding behind the damn bushes to attack me while I'm pregnant. You're real proud about that shit. You got your chest poked out. Bitch, please! Wait until I have this baby. Best believe, you will get yours." No matter what Alexis said, I would not back down to her, causing her to get angrier.

"I don't know where you live, how could I have fucked you up?"

"Bitch, don't be stupid. If you got my phone number, you got my address. You scratched Marcus car, remember that? Grow up and be a woman. Fight me one-on-one, after I have this baby. Oh yeah, you can only fight when you're hiding behind the bushes, covered in black. But that's not a fight, that's an attack, you bitch ass slut. I promise when I get my hands on you, it's all over."

I hung up the phone. Alexis continuously called my house. I stopped answering the phone and my mother called my cousins. I later found out, my Aunt Cheryl called Alexis pretending to be another girl. She thought if Alexis believed Marcus had another girlfriend, she would leave me alone. Alexis presumed it was my family calling her and she got scared.

My cousin, Shane called Alexis, acting as if he was just another guy interested in dating her, trying to get her to confess. They didn't want to kill someone, who indeed was innocent.

During the conversation, Alexis called her girlfriend, Tammy and they started bragging about knowing how to carry things out. My cousins had what they needed to make a move. With Alexis running her mouth so much, she confirmed that she and Tammy were responsible for burning me on November 16.

Unfortunately, heresy isn't enough for the police. Later that evening, my cousins arrived at my house and called her again. We put her on the speaker phone to hear the conversation.

Cool took the initiative to call. "Alexis, This is Cool. What's going on with you and Keacha?"

In her sweetest bi-polar voice, Alexis says, "Hey Cool. I don't know what's going on with your cousin. I heard she got fucked up pretty bad. You know she got a lot of enemies."

"Naw, Alexis I didn't know that. Why would she have a lot of enemies? You're the only person she's having a problem with?

Her voice started getting louder, "See that's the problem, y'all don't know Keacha or Lady or whatever y'all call her, like that. That bitch is into a lot of shit. She thinks she's all that. I'm glad she got burned. She deserved everything she got. I'm glad she got fucked up. She should be glad WE didn't do more than that." Then she caught herself.

My cousin, Shane, yelled out, "Bitch, you just messed up. You said WE!"

Alexis got real quiet and didn't say anything. She was terrified.

Shane said, "You're fuckin' with the wrong family. We gon' handle this and you can take that to the bank." He slams the phone down and turns to Cool, "I hope she got her kids out of the house, 'cuz we 'bout to blow this bitch up."

I tried to convince my cousins to leave it alone. They were ready to take her out and I kept pleading with them not to kill her. I knew that God wouldn't be pleased. I made him a promise. I was looking out for my little girl. What if they killed her and my daughter died. At this point, I knew God was real and I couldn't renege on a promise. I kept telling them, what comes around goes around; she would pay for what she did. Don't worry about it. Let the police handle it. I didn't want anybody in my family to go down with her. No matter how much I pleaded with them. It was a done deal. Alexis ignited a war, she couldn't end. My cousins stormed out of the house, like an army on a mission.

I called Detective Vaughn the next morning and told him about the telephone calls. He said, "Okay." A few minutes later, the doorbell rang. It was the police stating a girl called complaining about me playing on her phone. Fortunately, the officers remembered me from November 16. After I explained what was happening, they didn't look into it any further. I went back to my mother's house.

The following weekend, I had a baby shower planned. With all that was happening, I wasn't sure if I should have it or if anyone would come. Nevertheless, I decided Alexis wasn't going to ruin my baby shower. I continued with my plans.

To keep from attracting her, we didn't put the baby shower sign outside. Little did I know, Alexis was a constant visitor on my block, and she knew about the baby shower, in spite of us not displaying the sign.

Tracy decorated the house beautifully and bought me a nice wig, so I would look half decent. My skin was slowly getting back to normal. The swelling went down on my face. A black scar remained across my forehead and small scratches covered my entire face, but I didn't look as atrocious as I looked in the hospital.

My breasts were severely damaged because my bra held in the chemicals, causing third degree burns. The skin on my breast had disintegrated, and the flesh was swelling and blistering. I put dressing on the flesh to help with the healing, but it was very painful and had a horrible odor. My hair was burned out and would need to be shaved to re-grow evenly.

To my surprise, most of my friends and family attended the baby shower. People walked through the door cheerfully, bringing gifts. For the first time in weeks, I laughed and had fun; until Marcus came into the house and whispered, "Alexis' ex-boyfriend's gold Altima is parked at the end of our block."

Instead of ruining the party, I ignored him and continued with the celebration. The doorbell rang. It was the same two policemen who visited a few days earlier. They were trying to motion for me

NOT to open the door, but I didn't understand. According to the policemen, Alexis called and told them she had a warrant for my arrest.

She was watching the house to see if I would get arrested. The officers were really nice, told me to enjoy my party and save them a plate. I pretended everything was normal, but my mother kept asking who was at the door. I burst into tears. Alexis managed to ruin my baby shower anyway.

I told everyone Alexis was in the neighborhood, watching the house and trying to have me arrested during the baby shower. I also told them what Marcus said about the gold Altima being at the top of the block. Three of the guys who were at the baby shower, Norman, Chris and Trey stormed out of the house, circling the block looking for the gold Altima.

Marcus had left to pick up his mother and grandmother. He should have told the guys, as soon as he saw the car. What did he think I was going to do? At least the men could have beaten the shit out of Alexis. At that time, she deserved it. The gold Altima had disappeared by the time they went to search for it.

December 18, the baby's due date, seemed too far away. With three weeks remaining and a warrant out for my arrest, I stayed at my mother's apartment, even on the weekends, praying Alexis still did not have my mother's address.

On December 13, 2000, I had my beautiful daughter, *Kaylah Alexiz*. Kaylah spelled with an "h" is a Hebrew name meaning *one who is like God*. A beautiful round face baby, with curly black hair, Kaylah had the fattest cheeks with the cutest clef in her chin. I was so happy she was healthy, and had all of her limbs. From the stress of the pregnancy, I feared my baby might have problems. Other than a dark spot that covered a small part of her face (closer to her headline), she was absolutely perfect, weighing seven pounds and eight ounces. I was overjoyed because my baby was safe. Now it was time to focus on kicking Alexis' ass.

After feeding the baby and laying her in the hospital bassinet, the telephone rang.

"Hello," I said.

"Bitch, you're going to die!" I hung up the phone. *How did she know what hospital I was in and my room number?*

I called my mother and we got security involved. No one could visit my room without an ID and approval. There was no way Alexis could get into the hospital room, without being caught. During the entire stay, Alexis constantly called the hospital room. Becoming annoyed, I took the phone off of the hook, preventing others who wanted to say congratulations from calling.

At this point, no one knew where Alexis was hiding. She was not at her apartment or her mother's house, which my cousins staked out, but decided not to bomb, to avoid killing Alexis' mother in the revenge.

After having the baby, I decided I was going home and this time I was staying. I worked hard to buy my house, so hiding from Alexis was no longer permitted. As soon as I got home, the phone calls continued. The phone rang all night long. I woke up one night and saw the message light blinking on the indicator. I told Marcus to listen to the message.

It was the "Clean Up Man" again saying, "So you 'bout it 'bout it now. I got your lil message. We gonna handle that."

There were two more messages with a disgruntled female, rapping about shooting and killing. To our surprise, after the messages finished playing, the machine proudly repeated the telephone number that delivered the messages, 410-955-5555. "That's her telephone number," Marcus confirmed. *I thought you didn't know her new home number.*

We tape recorded the messages, along with her telephone number and planned to call Detective Vaughn and Detective Shaw in the morning. At last, we had evidence Alexis Mason was harassing us.

Detective Vaughn was not available again, so Detective Shaw called the number and indeed spoke with Alexis. Afterwards, he called me and said Alexis told him we were fighting over Marcus. She told Detective Shaw I called her house as well.

I was furious. He actually believed what she said. I started yelling, "I'm the one who was brutally beaten but, you think I'm playing on her phone."

"Maybe Marcus should clear this up," he suggested.

"What the hell do I need the police department for? I'm trying to do the right thing and you're telling me Marcus should handle it. Are you serious? This is ridiculous! You are actually having a conversation with the woman who assaulted and burned me, and you won't pick her up."

"Miss Jones, we are working on your case."

"Yeah, right," I ended the conversation.

The next day, I tried to listen to the messages again. They were erased. I called Marcus.

"Did you erase the messages from the phone system?"

"No, why?"

"They have been erased."

"What? That's impossible. Call the telephone company."

I called the telephone company. "Ms. Jones, we just spoke with you. You told us to reset your answering machine because you forgot the password."

I was devastated, Alexis called the telephone company pretending to be me and had the messages erased. Luckily, we had them on a tape. However, that meant she had my personal information and knew enough about me to convince the telephone operator she was me.

Marcus was under a lot of stress. He felt responsible and was petrified. He stood by the door all night long, watching Alexis and a white van drive past my house every night. The white van drove pass my house, slowing down to surveillance the door. Then, it circled the block several times repeating the same actions. The windows were tinted so we couldn't see who was driving. Alexis' lil black car followed behind the van. I don't know what their plans were, but I knew I had to be prepared.

I had my .357 magnum and Marcus started carrying a big knife around. Whenever we left the house, I had the gun and he had a knife. I was afraid that the gun would fall out or we would get caught. In Baltimore City, carrying a gun was an automatic five years in jail. However, I was determined to shoot anybody else who tried to harm me, especially since the detectives did absolutely nothing to help me.

Enough was enough. I needed to get law enforcement more involved, since I blocked my family from killing Alexis. Marcus and I set off to the police station and told them what was happening. We wanted to talk to anyone who would listen. We were getting nowhere with the detectives. They had not shown me any mug shots of possible suspects. They did not interview Alexis or give her a lie detector test. They did absolutely nothing to find the culprits who assaulted and burned me on November 16.

The commissioner told me to fill out a charging document. The four-page report contained all of the harassment I had been experiencing from Alexis. The commissioner promised Alexis would be charged and arrested on assault.

On December 19, I was in the process of having all of my hair shaved, when Alexis started calling again. She found out there was a second warrant issued for her arrest and she was livid. My sister, Angie and her husband Chris were visiting. Angie answered the phone and started arguing with Alexis. I told Angie to hang up the telephone until I finished getting my hair cut. Alexis called back and I answered.

"You are going to die tonight, bitch!" she said.

"Bitch! How many times are you going to say that? Bring it! I've been waiting for this day for three months."

As Angie and Chris were leaving, a guy in all black came from nowhere and startled them. Chris pulled out his gun and the guy took off running.

I sent my children to my mother's house and waited for Alexis that night. Tracy and Norman came over again. We watched from the bedroom window as the white van kept circling the house.

We planned to catch Alexis when she drove down the street, like she did every night around 10:00 pm.

This time, we planned to throw a chair in front of the car to stop it, drag her out of the car into the house, and beat her to death. With her record of coming to my house, police would believe she came to my house again and got caught. We had guns, knives, and bats in the house waiting to do some damage. To get her stirred up, we called her telephone number through the answering machine and replayed the recording with her messages and telephone number on it. To our surprise, Alexis didn't come around that night. Nothing happened.

The next morning, we all got dressed to leave. Marcus left first. A few minutes later Marcus returned with three police officers behind him. The police officers had a warrant for my arrest. I started crying. Everybody tried to explain what was going on with Alexis. The police officer told Marcus he needed to stay away from me, since he was causing these types of problems.

The police officers did not call the paddy wagon or handcuff me. They also had no idea what the warrant said. The only information they knew; a girl was picked up last night. She told them she had a warrant on me and gave them my address. This meant Alexis and I would be in jail together. She was the girl picked up last night, preventing her from stalking me that night, and getting beat to death.

I was terrified of going to jail. I had never been to jail or visited a jail before, but I refused to show any fear walking in threw the prison doors. The police officer handcuffed me when we got to the front door, since all criminals should be handcuffed upon arrest. As soon as I walked in, they took the handcuffs off. The officer requested that Alexis and I stay separated. Through the door, there was a desk, a hall with about three cells on each side, and a search room.

I glanced up and saw Alexis' evil eyes staring at me with a smirk on her face. This was the second time; I was face to face with this evil manipulating bitch. It took all I had to stare her down until she turned away. I wanted her to know I was not afraid of her.

The correctional officers escorted me into a small room for a cavity search. I was told to remove all my clothes, including my wig. When the officers saw my chest, they said, "Oh, my God! What happened to you?"

I explained what Alexis did. The cavity search was so humiliating, especially since I was still bleeding from having my baby one week ago. As I got dressed, the officers said I could not put my wig back on.

Walking out of the room without my wig, all eyes were on me. Somebody yelled, "Damn!" Everybody burst into laughter, especially Alexis.

Holding my head up, I walked over to get fingerprinted and photographed. I refused to allow her to get the best of me. My hair was shaved off into a low cut fade, so I wore the wig. After removing the wig, they all saw the real deal. Had it not been shaved the previous day, I would have been even more embarrassed.
I got my warrant papers and it read……

The above defendant LaKeacha Michelle Jones had her cousin by the name of Dante call my home. The phone was answered by my mother. He asked if he could speak to Marcus. My mother told him that Marcus did not live here. Then Dante said that he was Keacha's cousin and he was looking for Alexis, Marcus' daughter's mother. My mother kindly explained to him that Marcus and I had no dealings with one another, so please don't call her house again. After moments later, the phone rang again. Therefore, I answered it only to be surprised by LaKeacha Jones on the other end. I asked her why she was calling me playing on my phone. She then said, "Bitch, don't worry about it. When I see your dumb ass, I am going to fucking kill you. I'm going to smash your ass, just like I did your car. Fuck you and your daughter. I should have fucked you up while you were pregnant so that little bastard would not be here now. But that's okay. I'm going to throw a fucking bomb in your house and kill everybody so you better watch your fucking back because when I'm through with you, you will not be recognized." After that, her cousin got back on the phone and said, "Bitch, you better get your fucking daughter out of the house because I'm going to blow that shit up." I do not want to take threats lightly because of what happened to my car and from previous phone calls, approximately 18 calls thereafter. I fear for my life and the life of my two-month old daughter and I can't afford to have her taken away from me, or vice versa because of LaKeacha Jones' actions. I know it was Ms. Jones because she stated to me who she was and I am familiar with her voice. After the calls, I was very scared and shaken up because of this.

I was astonished. Everything written on those charging documents was false. How could they arrest me for this? This was heresy and a complete lie. This proved she had all of my identity information. She knew the correct spelling of my full name and she knew my birthday.

So many things in this document identified her as the assailant on November 16. The statements like, "She had her cousin by the name of Dante call my home." I don't have a cousin named Dante. However, on November 16, the guy asked for Dante, when he broke into my house.

She also wrote I said to her, "I should have fucked you up while you were pregnant, so that little bastard would not be here now." Is it a coincidence that's exactly what happened to me?

Furthermore, she wrote that I said, "When I'm through with you, you will not be recognized." Was this another coincidence? I don't think so; the way my face looked on November 16, I was not recognized.

Everything she wanted to say to me and had been telling me through her phone calls, Alexis wrote in her charging documents, pretending *I* said them to her. Alexis manipulated the charging documents to make it seem like I was the harasser and she was the victim. Therefore, if anything happened to her, there would be a record of my threats to her. This girl was evil, insane and devious.

The correctional officers placed me in a cell directly across from Alexis. She continued staring at me. I didn't back down. I kept my eyes on her until I heard, "Bitch, what the fuck are you looking at?"

This big black lady in my cell got up and started cussing at Alexis. The woman and her daughter had been fighting and both got arrested. The daughter was in the cell with Alexis. The woman assumed Alexis was staring at her, instead of me and cussed Alexis out. After that, Alexis went and sat down in the corner. Guess she wasn't so tough after all.

I wanted to cry, but I couldn't let her see me crying. She hated me and I hated her more. Sometimes, I couldn't stop the tears. I was angry and trapped. *All of this because of Marcus, the good guy. What the hell is happening to me? Why didn't I leave him in the beginning? How did I let it go this far?*

The cell was horrible. There was a toilet, made of steel, two steel benches, a cement floor and sliding bars. Women of all kinds were in there: several crack heads, one drug dealer, the mother that was fighting her daughter, a pretty girl whose boyfriend wrote a warrant on her and a light-skinned gay lady. They talked and fussed, but I said nothing. Breakfast came by; I didn't eat. The crack heads grabbed my food and ate it.

Lunch came around; I still didn't eat. The prisoner who served the food said, "Shorty, you need to eat."

I wasn't about to eat that jail food. I looked over at Alexis, who was eating like a hungry beast.

I waited to see the commissioner, and then I would get my phone call to my mother. Around 4:00 in the afternoon, we moved to another cell, closer to the commissioner's office. A girl sat next to me and started asking me why I was in there. I told her about the false report Alexis had written. Alexis walked by and winked her eye at the girl. They started laughing. I immediately stopped talking to her. She had befriended Alexis and was trying to get information from me. On her way back from the commissioner's office, Alexis wasn't smiling anymore, she was shaking her head, looking infuriated.

When, I arrived at the commissioners, station, a female commissioner read the charging documents and said, "Y'all fighting over a man? Y'all need to stop. You're a teacher, acting like this."

I tried to explain, but she didn't care. She set the bail for $10,000. I needed $1,000 to get out. I had a court scheduled for January 19, 2001. When the correctional officer came to escort me back to the cell, he asked about my bail. I told him. He said, "You alright, Shorty? Your girl got $50,000 bail."

I called my mom to tell her what my bail was. Norman had gotten me a lawyer and was coming to release me, as soon as possible. We all had to go upstairs to get uniforms and a dorm bed. A female correctional officer reminded the male correctional officer to keep me and Alexis separated. The male correctional officer responded, "They ain't gonna fight," and started laughing. The correctional officers acted worse than some of the inmates. I concluded there was no professionalism in the prison system. Correctional officers and common criminals were synonymous.

Alexis walked directly behind me, as we moved upstairs. I started walking slower and slower. I was thinking, *Touch me please. Please touch the hem of my garment, so I can beat the shit outta you. This is it. This is the day; I get to take all my anger out on her. I'm going to let her make the first move. Then I'm going to beat her until she's breathless.*

I wanted to turn around and beat Alexis to a pulp. I had endured enough and was already in the worst place possible. I hoped she would bump into me or step on my shoe, so I could have a reason to whoop her ass and claim self-defense. I could feel all of my strength building up to beat the shit out of her.

I was already in jail and didn't want to make things worse for myself. However, fucking her up would have been worth whatever punishment I received. Needless to say, she caught on and stayed far behind me. She could have gotten the best of me from behind but, she knew I was waiting to fuck her up.

We went to a big room to get a prison uniform. I called my mother again and sat on the bench. Alexis had the audacity to come sit next to me. "Keacha, we need to talk. This doesn't make any sense. All of this over a man."

Remaining calm, I said, "Bitch, you have crossed the line and you're steady digging a grave for yourself."

"Well, my lawyer has my telephone records, right now, so I'm going to walk."

"Alexis, I am about two seconds from beating the shit out of you. You attacked me when I was pregnant, so now you think I'm a punk. You act like this is a game and you wanna have a sit down and talk. Bitch, please. This is my life you're playing with. I advise you to get the fuck away from me." I didn't yell, but the intensity in my voice told her I was serious as a heart attack. She moved away and didn't say anything else to me. *Yeah bitch, what happened to all that mouth you had on the phone?*

Alexis started talking to the other inmates, pretending to be hardcore, talking about how much weed she smoked and how she missed her little mama, Marcus' daughter. I called my mother, one last time to ensure everything was being taken care of and I would be out soon. Alexis made her phone calls outside of the big room, so I wouldn't hear her conversation. She needed $5,000. She didn't have a job, so her mother would have to put up her house. I could see through her faking; she was scared as hell.

Dinner came around. I still didn't eat. Again, she was eating like a hungry animal. Nothing I saw of Alexis justified why Marcus was with her. She was either a hell of a lover or he loved the drama she brought into his life. She was classless, ghetto and straight hood. We were nothing alike. In her pretending, she wanted to be like me, but there was absolutely no way, he could compare Alexis Mason to me. For him to admit he loved us both, he had to be insane. If he could love someone like that, there was definitely a mental issue that needed to be addressed. Still I ignored the signs.

In the dorm room, the light-skinned gay lady started asking me about what was going on between me and that girl. Remembering from the last conversation, I told her a short version, not wanting to be tricked again.

She was cool though. She said, "You don't look like you did what she said you did. You've been quiet all day and she runs her mouth all the time. You can tell a lot about a person by watching them. You seem to be quiet and mind your business, but that bitch is crazy. She did that stuff to you?" she asked, pointing to the scars on my face.

I said, "Yeah."

"Why did you cut your hair off?" she asked.

"My hair was burned out when she poured the chemicals on me."

"When you came in here I said, Awww shucks, we got Patti Labelle up in here. I was waiting for you to break out singing, *Somebody Love Me, Baby*. Then you came out bald and I was like DAMN!"

She was the big mouthed person that caused everybody to laugh at me. I started smiling.

She said, "You know what? What comes around goes around. You will be alright." God has angels in all types of places. I went home around 10:00 pm. Marcus and Norman picked me up. I was starving, so I went to my mother's house to eat.

That day was the first time in eight years I missed my son's birthday, December 20, 2000. He didn't mention it. My mother bought him a cake and they sang Happy Birthday. I promised to take him to Toys R Us and buy him some video games. That made him happy.

I changed my telephone number and went back home to enjoy Christmas with my family. I was still determined not to let Alexis run me away from my house. Getting arrested must have frightened her because she didn't call or come around, for the remaining of the year.

CHAPTER 6: WE'RE MARRIED NOW

"More marriages might survive if the partners realize that sometimes the better comes after the worse."
Doug Larson

It had been an entire year, since the saga with Alexis Mason had begun. I had been attacked with a bat, kicked while pregnant, burned with chemicals at my new house, and then falsely arrested by the same person who burned me. In one year, my life went from cosmos to chaotic.

Marcus and I slept through the entire New Year's Eve celebration. We didn't have much to be happy about because of everything that was going on. I was still on maternity leave and had been out of work since November 16. All of my bills were behind, because I had to pay the lawyer and the bail bond to get out of jail. I was so stressed out. I couldn't focus on paying bills and keeping everything up. My finances started falling behind.

My mother started pressuring Marcus and me to get married. I wanted to get married to Marcus, but I never really thought it would happen, especially that quick. I didn't have an opinion on the matter. My mother kept saying, "Y'all need to get married." Her logic was I wouldn't be just another "baby's mother" when we went to court. I would be his wife.

Marcus wasn't ready for marriage, but his guilt was taking over and he didn't want any more problems with my family. He called me on January 9th and said, "We're getting married tomorrow."

"Okay," I said.

This definitely wasn't the proposal I saw on TV and envisioned for myself. There was no ring, no bending on one knee and no romance. Marcus seemed to be fine with it, but that was not my ideal of a proposal.

The following day, we got dressed up and went to the Baltimore County Courthouse. I was wearing a white church suit my mother had given me and a long wrap wig. Marcus had on a black suit. We didn't invite anyone, it was just us. Chris had given Marcus an old engagement ring he had for some other chick, and I bought Marcus a thin band from the pawn shop. We intended to purchase real rings later.

The ceremony room was set up very attractively. There were floral arrangements around the room, beautiful white chairs and the alter was splendidly decorated.

The officiate asked Marcus, "Will you love, honor, comfort, and cherish LaKeacha from this day forward, forsaking all others, keeping only unto her for as long as you both shall live?"

Marcus and I held hands, and looked into each other eyes. "I will," he responded.

"Do you take Marcus to have and to hold from this day forward, for better or for worse, for richer, for poorer, in sickness, in health, to love and to cherish; and promise to be faithful until death part you?"

"I will." *I guess I'm doing the right thing.* The officiate asked for the rings and we repeated, "With this ring, I thee wed." Marcus placed the ring on my finger and I placed the thin gold band on his finger.

"You may now kiss the bride."

That's it. Where are the sparkles and the fireworks? I couldn't explain the feeling I had. I thought I was happy and wanted to be married to Marcus, but at that moment, it didn't seem right. We were forced into a marriage because of the situation. I didn't feel like a true bride.

Regardless, I was now married to Marcus. We planned to have a real wedding later that year. We left the court house and had lunch at City Lights, my other favorite restaurant.

Although quiet, Alexis was still on the prowl. We were missing important telephone messages from our lawyer. When we tried to retrieve our messages, the response system said, "This mailbox is currently in use by another party." We realized Alexis got into our answering machine and was listening, then deleting our messages. Marcus changed the password.

Alexis and I both had to be in court on January 19, 2001 for an arraignment. Arraignment is a criminal proceeding, in which the defendant is officially called before the judge. After reviewing the charges the judge will determine if the case proceeds to trial or is dismissed. The Courthouse was located in East Baltimore on North Avenue.

Most of my cousins attended court with me. If anything was going down that day, we were prepared. We separated ourselves to avoid her recognizing anyone. I knew my cousins would keep an eye on her, especially Norman. Since she was hiding and no one knew where she was staying, Norman planned to follow her after court, to get a current location.

Marcus, Tracy, and my mother were sitting next to me. Alexis sashayed into the courtroom with a posse of girls, then stood on the side of the wall; lurking, plotting her next move. I glanced to see if one of the girls was the third culprit on November 16, but I didn't recognize any of them.

"The State of Maryland vs. Alexis Mason." the court clerk called. Alexis pleaded not guilty. The judge reviewed my complaint and told her that she would go to trial for 1st and 2nd degree assault and was facing 25 years in jail.

"Yes!" I shrieked in excitement. As Alexis exited the courtroom, gazing my way, I smiled. "Bitch! she responded." I gave her the birdie.

A few cases later, I was called to the front of the courtroom. "The State of Maryland vs. LaKeacha Jones." I was confident that my case would be dismissed. The complaint was totally false and ridiculous. Anybody with a brain could read that document and perceive it to be non-sense. Besides, the alleged victim had just walked out of the courtroom. Within five minutes the judge announced. "This case is dismissed. Next!" Finally, I got some justice.

As I was leaving the courtroom, Detective Vaughn started talking to me about the case. Where was he the entire two months since I had been burned? He showed absolutely no interest in the case before, and all of a sudden, he wanted to have a conversation.

"How can I help you, Detective Vaughn?"

"We have some leads on your case. We think it was Alexis Mason, but we need some concrete evidence."

"And you want me to do what, Detective? Find you some evidence?" I said sarcastically.

"Ms. Jones."

"It's Mrs. Jett, now."

"Oh, uh, congratulations. When can we meet with the states attorney to discuss the case?"

"Whenever you are ready, I will be available." I walked away. I was fed up with the detectives and their attitude towards my case. I was a victim. No matter what their thoughts were about Marcus and me, it was their responsibility to solve the case or attempt to find out who assaulted me.

The perpetrator was delivered to them on a platter, yet they allowed her to manipulate the legal system and play mindless games with my life. From the detectives' behaviors, I can understand why some people took the law into their own hands. In order for the detectives to show some interest in my case, I needed to get shot or killed, which I'm sure was next on psycho Alexis' list.

We met with the State's Attorney about my case. "LaKeacha, I must be honest with you. There are some discrepancies with your case. From the report I have, the police officer on scene said that you told her there were two men and one person dressed in black that you could not identify." I listened.

"Furthermore, the detectives stated you did not know if Alexis Mason was involved."

"Are you fucking kidding me?" I yelled. "I told everyone from day one that it was Alexis Mason. I told the officer that night. I told the detectives that Saturday morning it was her. I called them over and over again, telling them she was still harassing me. Y'all fucked up and now you want to place the blame on me."

"Calm down, Ms. Jones." said the State's Attorney. "You were delusional that night. You may not have known what you said."

"I know what the hell I said. I know who did this to me. I am a teacher, not a drug dealer. I don't have people attempting to kill me for no reason. So if it wasn't her, who was it? Maybe it was one of my second grade students, who came to my house and burned me with chemicals. Then again, maybe it probably was one of their parents. Yeah that's it. Oh, I have one better. Maybe it was a random act of violence. Three people just so happen to walk down my quiet, secluded street, rung my bell, and beat the shit out of me for no apparent reason. Is that what you think? All along while, Alexis Mason is the one who kicked me in my stomach while I was six months pregnant, threatened she was going to kill me, stalked me, called and harassed me and wrote false police reports on me, but it wasn't her. This is some bullshit! I will handle it myself." I stood up to leave.

"Ms. Jones. Sit down."

"It's Mrs. Jett and I am done with this foolishness."

"Give us some time to do more research. We are going to test the glove that Marcus found to determine if we can get any DNA from it. I will call you in a few weeks to let you know our findings."

I was livid with the outcome of that meeting. The detectives lied about several things. They alleged that they questioned Alexis, but they never did. They said I told them I didn't know if the attacker was Alexis, which certainly was a lie. At least, we had a glove that could be used as evidence. I was positive Alexis had the glove on, while she poured the chemicals on me and tried to cover my mouth, as I was screaming. She may have been burning from the chemicals and discarded the glove, as she was running. I have no idea how the glove got on the side of the stairs, nevertheless, we had some evidence.

I went back to work February 4, 2001. I was petrified, but I needed to get out of the house and make some money. I had a feeling Alexis would attempt to kill me the next time she attacked. Going to and coming from work, was the only time I was alone. Alexis would never fight me one-on-one, and I could not beat a group of goons, no matter what. However, I could shoot their asses, so I carried my .357 to school every day.

When I was with Antoine, I was around all types of guns, 9 mm, pistols, AK47's, but I never shot a gun. I barely held one. I could hear Antoine saying, "Ma, if anybody come up on you, shoot first, ask questions later. If you want peace, keep your piece." I never thought the day would come when I would have to carry around a gun for protection.

Once I got into the building, I made sure it was in a safe and secure place. If the gun ever fell out or was noticed, I would lose my job and be sent to Baltimore City jails, no questions asked.

My students and parents were elated I was back at work. My principal was informed of the situation and was very understanding. Thankfully, he didn't reveal to the staff the details of my assault, so no one knew what was going on. He also allowed me to use my new name, hoping to deter uninvited guest from getting into my room.

It would have been very easy for Alexis to come into the building as a parent and try something crazy, but my principal had the school secured. There were video cameras on every hall and stairwell. In addition, he called to check on me throughout the week and allowed me to keep the classroom door locked, although it was against policy. I told my students they were not allowed to open the door and everyone had to be screened by me.

During this time, I noticed Alexis' small black car parked across the street from the school. As soon as she realized I spotted her, she pulled off. The next day, she would park in a different spot, sitting and staring. She parked too far to attack me, but close enough to watch my every move. I imagined she was waiting for the perfect opportunity to shoot me.

To make it known of her presence, she stole my Mercedes Benz sign, out of the circle that stood on the top of the hood. I was driving home one afternoon when I noticed something different. I said, "What the fuck happened to the Benz sign?" It was completely removed. All that remained was an empty circle.

Arriving to my neighborhood, Alexis parked on Northern Parkway, adjacent to my street, so she could spot me when I turned onto my street. Again, by the time I saw her and made a U-turn, she disappeared.

I could not explain how Alexis found the time to keep track of my every move. She had two children to take care of and a job she needed to find; but she made monitoring me, a part of her daily life. She obviously had set her schedule to observe me going to work, almost every morning and spy on me every afternoon, as I arrived home.

The stress that I endured was unbelievable. The anxiety and constant worrying caused the night terrors to increase. I woke up screaming and crying at least three times a week. I didn't know when I would be killed, jumped or arrested.

I wasn't afraid of Alexis, by any means. She had proven, time and time again, she was a punk. The fact that she got other people involved, and there was no way for me to determine who was a part of her schemes, is what tortured me. So I trusted no one, I didn't know. I wondered what Alexis told people, to get them caught up in harassing me. Although my girlfriends were ride or die chicks, I couldn't imagine them stalking someone with me, just because I didn't like the person or because the other person had something I wanted.

Not knowing when these "unknown people" would pop off and the repeated false reports, Alexis wrote to have me arrested, are the reasons I lived in fear. If I heard someone walking up the steps, I got nervous. Every time, the doorbell rang, I hid for fear it would be the police officers coming to arrest me again. If I left the house alone, I returned before the sun went down. Nervousness and anxiety took over anytime I approached the house. I would call Marcus and ask him to stand at the door, while I scurried inside.

Tension, worry, concern and fear are the ingredients for anxiety attacks. The first time I had an anxiety attack, I thought I was having a stroke. My body got numb and wouldn't move. My face was twisted. No sounds came out of my mouth. I couldn't scream or call for help, so calling 911 was out of the question. I made several trips to the emergency room. Finally a doctor put me on Paxil, a drug used to treat depression, panic disorder, and social anxiety disorder. Used to help with sudden, unexpected attacks of extreme fear and worry about these attacks or extreme fear of interacting with others, Paxil became my best friend.

Marcus was so patient and loving. I could see the pain in his eyes. When I woke up crying, he held me and rocked me until I fell asleep. He sat up with the baby all night until she fell asleep. He took me to every lawyer and state's attorney visit. He listened as much as I talked. He was sincerely sorry, but he didn't know how to fix the problem, without committing murder.

Marcus had not seen his daughter since the day he brought her to my house in November. Although Alexis continued calling him and emailing him, he didn't talk to her. He contacted Child Support Enforcement so he could start making payments before Alexis initiated the request, but the representative told him, the mother of the child, had to request child support. After continuous calls from Alexis, Marcus finally wrote her a letter:

Alexis,
DO NOT – I repeat – DO NOT send me anymore email messages. Because of what you have done, are doing and probably what you plan to do, I want nothing to do with you. In the event that our daughter wants to contact me when she is older and able to communicate on her own, she can feel free to contact me. Until then, I do not expect to open any emails from you. Marcus

To relieve some of our stress, Marcus and I took a trip to Atlantic City, NJ for the day. Atlantic City proved to be a much needed break from all the stress and drama. We walked on the boardwalk, visited some museums and other cultural attractions. We gambled a little, hoping to hit something to pay our overextending bills. Afterwards, we strolled the beach.

We made a rule to not discuss Alexis Mason or anything concerning her. Instead, we enjoyed each other's company and savored the much needed peace, wishing it could last forever.

Reality kicked in as we arrived home. There was another letter from the court. I was charged again, but not arrested. A new court date was set for March 6, 2001. I didn't have a clue of what was going on.

On Monday, my lawyer informed me that Alexis had written another warrant to have me arrested. The words were the exact same as the first warrant. Thankfully, instead of arresting me, the judge issued a court date. This time I had to bring letters of support from my family and friends to prove, I was not the malicious person in this love triangle. Instead of inviting my family, Marcus and I arrived at court alone. Alexis didn't show up again, so the charges were dismissed.

Although I was glad the charges were dismissed, I was enraged that someone could write charging documents to have someone else arrested (or summoned for court) and NOT appear in court. I spent a lot of unnecessary money for a lawyer and missed a day from work, because of her spitefulness.

I questioned one of the police officers at the courtroom and he told me that was the way it was in Baltimore City. There were no consequences for writing complaints or applications of charges and not appearing for court. *This is ludicrous!* I began writing letters to the Mayor, the Commissioner, the City Council and the news stations. I also wrote letters to the police commissioners to complain about the actions of the detectives working my case. To my surprise, all of them responded, but none of them said anything to help.

At this time, Marcus and I noticed we weren't getting any mail for days. Mail that usually arrived in one day, such as paperwork from the lawyers office and court, we never received. "Someone" started stealing our mail. We replaced the regular mailbox with a sturdy key lock mailbox to stop the thief. In spite of our efforts, the thief was persistent about stealing the mail.

When we arrived home in the evening, envelopes were pulled all the way to the top of the mailbox and torn, as if someone was trying to get it through the locked mail slot. Marcus and I decided to put up a video camera to catch the mail thief, Alexis, on our porch stealing mail. We were excited we had come up with this bright idea to finally prove, Alexis Mason was the one stalking me over the last year.

Every time we observed the mail had been tampered with, the video camera either disconnected or the picture would be shuttering and we couldn't see anyone. We spent our entire evenings watching the video tape, trying to catch her. We never did.

By now, she had my social security number, court papers, medical bills and other vital information that came through the mail. Marcus wrote a letter to the post office to inform them of the theft. We opened a post office box and had our mail rerouted.

At this time, we were awaiting trial for the incident with Alexis and the bat. If this case appeared in court before the second case appeared in court, we would have solid evidence of Alexis' notorious behavior against me, and it would lay a concrete foundation for the second case. Because of this knowledge, Alexis' lawyer requested multiple postponements.

It was important for us to get mail from the court to keep abreast of the cases. It was equally important for Alexis to steal the mail because if we missed a court date, the bat case against her would be dismissed, leading the way for the burning incident to be dismissed against her as well.

God watches over fools and babies. It must be true. Surely, God was protecting Alexis and didn't want her to be caught. Nothing we tried worked. As soon as we put up the video camera, she stopped stealing the mail. It amazed me how Alexis knew so much about what was going on in our lives. She got away with everything she did. Her knowledge of the criminal system was impeccable. She knew how to maneuver the system to her benefit. Maybe her previous job as a correctional officer trained her to be a certified criminal.

The promise I made to God stayed fresh on my mind, but the only way I was going to stop Alexis from ruining my life was to kill her. Getting married to Marcus didn't faze her one bit. Even if I left Marcus, Alexis would continue to haunt me. She was determined to ruin my life, as if she had not done enough.

Despite the drama, Marcus and I went on our honeymoon in May to Las Vegas. We were so excited about our four day vacation. We needed to get some rest. In the five months of our marriage, we spent most of the time dealing with Alexis and the problems she caused.

The bills were still behind. However, spending money for this trip was essential to keeping our sanity. Once again, we promised ourselves we would not mention Alexis during the entire trip.

Las Vegas was indeed fabulous. After sleeping almost an entire day, Marcus and I cruised the strip, visiting all of the fancy hotels and casinos. Some of our family members and friends joined us on the trip, so we had parties at the pool and met for dinner at various restaurants. We ate. We laughed. We danced. We had the best time of our lives. Staying true to our word, we did not discuss Alexis the entire trip.

Coming home was very depressing. Our next court date was July 11, 2001, a few weeks away. My mother, aunt, Cousin Lamar, Marcus and I went with us to court. Alexis arrived at the courthouse with, another female, obviously a relative, judging by her appearances. As she did her usual parading through the courthouse, my cousin Lamar leaped out of his seat to grab her. My aunt and I held him back. We could not have him getting arrested in court. When the court clerk called her case, her lawyer asked for another postponement and it was granted. Alexis dashed out the courthouse, amused.

She hopped in her mother's gold Camry and started driving real slow in front of us. I was infuriated. I reached over Marcus and started blowing the horn, yelling out the window, "You stupid bitch!" All of a sudden, she slammed on brakes. Marcus pounded the brakes to keep from hitting her mother's car.

By then I had enough of her. *Fuck it. I'm going to jail because I'm gonna fuck her up.* I pulled off my heels and jumped out of the car, running towards her. My mother, aunt and Lamar all jumped out of the car. Alexis and her ugly sidekick stepped out of the car. My mother grabbed me.

"Let me go!" I was trying to get to Alexis. "You stupid bitch! I'm sick of your shit! Let me go mommy!" I screamed.

"Let her go mommy!" Alexis teased. "You wanna see me? Come around the way."

"Keacha, you know what she is trying to do," my mother said.

"No, bitch! I'm coming to your house. 1200 Davonport Court!" I yelled back at Alexis. She looked shocked I had called out her address. My mother loosened her grip and I ran for her. Both girls jumped back in the car and pulled off.

Marcus started driving. Alexis drove a little further, and then jumped out of the car again. We all exited the car, except Marcus. My aunt grabbed the bat (the same bat Alexis attacked me with) and went after her. Alexis hopped back into the car and sped up the highway.

We flagged down a police officer and told him what had just occurred. He told us we could file charges, although no physical harm was done. There was no sense in filing charges, so we left. Alexis was trying to get us to harm her, so the charges would be dropped against her, but she was too afraid of the beat down, so she ran.

Marcus never got out of the car. When everybody else jumped out, he sat there at the steering wheel. Later he said he was thinking about running her over.

When I got home, I called the state's attorney and told him about the incident. He said I needed to come to the office immediately. When I arrived the two detectives, along with the two states' attorneys were there. I asked them if I could tape record the conversation, but they said no because it could be used against them in a future lawsuit.

The state's attorney stated the DNA test was successful because it had undergone chemical testing. It was a positive match to the chemicals that were thrown on me. However, after the testing, there were not enough cells to test the glove for DNA. In addition, the police report and my warrant didn't match. The officer on the scene stated I did not know who the culprit was.

Detective Vaughn was enraged I had written a letter of complaint against him, so he started lying. He stated that he questioned my neighbors, which he didn't. He also said when he talked to me in the hospital; I was delirious and never mentioned a girl named Alexis.

Detective Shaw said he spoke with Alexis on the telephone and she told him we were fighting over Marcus. He sat with his head down. Most disturbing, Detective Vaughn said Marcus called him and told him Alexis was NOT involved in the incident. Marcus didn't respond.

I was livid. I started crying and accusing the detectives of a conspiracy. I told them they did not do their job and now they were trying to make me look like I was lying.

Detective Vaughn kept saying since I wrote a complaint on him, technically he didn't have to be there. Detective Shaw looked pathetic and didn't say anything. He knew Detective Vaughn was lying. They never questioned Alexis or her friend, Tammy, who may have been the light-skinned girl involved. The detectives never brought any pictures for me to identify the man out of the mug shots.

Every time I called Detective Vaughn, he told me he was a shooting detective and he had to put my case on the backlog. I couldn't understand why the police department would lie. What were they trying to hide? Were they friends with Alexis? Was she one of their correctional officer friends or was she their favorite stripper at the club?

The state's attorney was getting upset about Detective Shaw speaking with Alexis on the telephone. The state's attorney said he had Alexis' telephone records and she called me enough times to be considered telephone harassment. The tape recording we had could not be used against her because her voice was not on the recording, although the telephone number belonged to her.

The state's attorney said the case against Alexis would be dismissed because of insufficient evidence. Alexis was looking at 25 years, but I couldn't prove it was her. All I could do was file a telephone harassment complaint. There was no need for me to attend the next hearing, because they would contact her lawyer and tell her, the case was dismissed. If any evidence ever appeared that proved Alexis was involved with burning me that night, Alexis would be convicted for up to 25 years in jail, no matter how much time had passed. There was no statute of limitations on aggravated assault.

After this, I was physically and mentally exhausted. I didn't believe in the legal system anymore. They could not protect me from Alexis. She could do anything she wanted and get away with it. She knew how to work the legal system against me. I didn't know anything. I was a law abiding citizen and never would have imagined the legal system worked the way it did.

On July 19, 2001, as I was getting ready for work, the doorbell rang. I looked out of the window and saw police cars. I begged Marcus not to open the door. I called my mother and my supervisor and started crying again. Marcus opened the door anyway. I heard the officers talking to him.

Baltimore County Police had a warrant for my arrest. I was going to jail again. Alexis had written another false report on me. When they heard the story, they didn't take me in the paddy wagon; they drove me to Baltimore City Jail again, although the alleged crime happened in Baltimore County. This time, things had changed. The correctional officers were not allowed to do a cavity search.

This was her third false report against me. She wrote that on July 11, I jumped out of the car and attempted to hit her with a bat, but I missed. As I sat in the cell reading the charging documents, I could not believe, I was arrested for this. I could not understand how the law allowed people to write false charges, destroy somebody's life, and no punishment was given for not appearing in court.

I felt a bit of peace because I remembered Marcus saying if Alexis tried this again; he would take his chances and personally deal with her. As the drug addicts slept all over the cell, I sat in disbelief, waiting for my name to be called. When I saw the commissioner, he read the charges and said, "I think if you wanted to hit her with a bat, you would have hit her." Bail was set for $1,000. I only needed $100 to get out.

Marcus had the money to get me out. The only thing that kept me sane was thinking Marcus was going to kill Alexis. By this time, I didn't care. I wanted her dead. If I were in jail, they couldn't say I killed her. I ended up staying overnight in jail. The other women in the dorm tried to be supportive, but I didn't do anything to deserve what I was getting. Surprisingly, I had the most peaceful sleep in a long time.

The next morning, Marcus came to get me. He hugged me and I started crying again. After I calmed down, he said, "Now it's on."

What do you mean, NOW, it's on? It should be done. Alexis should be dead. You promised me that you would kill her if she tried this again.

Nothing was done to Alexis. I later found out Angie and my cousin Stephanie were going after her. Stephanie had a friend who promised to make Alexis disappear, with no traces that a murder ever occurred, but Marcus wouldn't give them her new address.

I was tired and drained. I had no peace in my spirit. I stopped going to work. I couldn't fight anymore. I needed to make a change so we decided to move to Delaware. We started packing the house and called the realtor to list it on the market. I explained to her why I needed to sell a house; I had not yet lived in a year.

At this time, we were also preparing for our wedding, planned for December. Between trying to move to Delaware, find a job and prepare for the wedding, Marcus and I were overwhelmed. We came home every evening and went straight to bed.

The state's attorney told me about The Witness Protection Program. He said they could help me move to Delaware. My mother and I went for an appointment in downtown Baltimore. I applied for the program, although I doubted it would be successful, since nothing else worked in my favor.

As we were leaving the office, engaged in our conversation, we crossed the street. BOOM! A loud bang and screeching sound was behind us. I looked back. A truck slammed into a car and the car was heading our way. I grabbed my mother's hand and yelled, "Run, Mommy!"

We sprinted down the sidewalk, with the car trailing behind us, but we didn't get very far. The car whacked both of us, knocking me at least 5 yards up the street. My mother was thrown into the wall, on the side of a bank building. I peered up and saw my mother lying on the hood of the car between the wall and the car. I started screaming loudly.

I didn't realize I was injured. I jumped up and ran to help my mother. Out of nowhere, people started helping and trying to calm me down. My mother whispered, "I'm alright." I was glad she was alive.

The ambulance rushed us to Mercy Hospital. The doctors couldn't believe we had such minor injuries compared to the accident report. I had a sprang ankle and a few bruises. My mother had a broken arm and a damaged hip.

We should have been dead. I knew the accident was a result of the voodoo Alexis put on my mother and me. But God is more powerful than any voodoo and I was still wearing my Star of David.

When Marcus arrived at the hospital, he couldn't believe what had occurred. He had been at child support court, where Alexis tried to sweet talk him and kept blowing him kisses. After all that happened, she was still determined to have Marcus. As far as I knew, he wasn't talking to her. He didn't see the baby and he showed no interest in her at all.

Why she continued to pursue him after a year, was beyond my knowledge. Alexis would send Marcus pictures of her in a sexy outfit, with her face covered. She sent emails and cards stating how much she loved him. She sent dozens of pictures of the baby to his grandmother's house, but never took the baby around them. She told Marcus' grandmother that she and I used to be friends and we hung out all the time. No such thing ever happened.

Marcus and I were still in the process of moving to Delaware, so I had a teaching interview scheduled for the following day. It had to be rescheduled because of the accident. Marcus requested a transfer from his job to Delaware. In the end, we decided rushing to Delaware wouldn't be a good idea without a job. So we moved in with my best friend, Tracy instead.

On August 1, 2001, We left my beautiful three bedroom house and moved in with Tracy. At first, it was okay because we were hardly there. We left early in the morning and came home late in the evening. I felt like a prisoner. I didn't feel comfortable with my entire family in someone else's house. I made sure I kept everything clean, didn't stay on the phone long, and tried not to be seen or heard. That was pretty hard to do with three children. Tracy didn't mind us being there and didn't ask for much in rent, but I still wasn't happy.

Our house was still on the market, but no one was interested in buying it. Marcus would go to the house and check on it, but I couldn't bring myself to go back. It frustrated me that I wasn't able to stay in my own house and live in peace and harmony.

On August 23, 2001, we went to the final court hearing against Alexis for the bat incident case. Everybody was getting tired of the court charades, so Angie, Marcus and I went to court. Nobody else attended. We weren't very optimistic about the case. So far, nothing had gone in our favor. We were sitting in the hall when Alexis came strolling through the courtroom, looking pissed, but trying to maintain her powerful image, but looking stupid. Her entourage was getting smaller and smaller. Even her ugly sidekick didn't come with her this time. When her case was called, she asked for a trial, so we had to testify. Marcus went to the car to get the bat she hit him with, as evidence.

They called Marcus to testify first. I had to sit in the hall, while he testified. When he came out, I went in to testify. I made sure I looked that evil, psychotic bitch directly in her face, as I told what happened. Since she got off for burning me on November 16, I was going to tell anything and everything I could tell about what she had put me through over the last year. I made sure to mention I was married to Marcus and Alexis was very jealous of our relationship. I made it clear after the bat incident; Alexis began stalking me, making harassing telephone calls, writing false police reports, and making my life miserable.

Alexis' defense attorney began to question me. I was ready for her, being that she saved Alexis from her much deserved jail time. She also lied and said Alexis was working on a criminal justice degree and was an apprentice in her law firm. Little did she know, she had been bamboozled by Alexis.

"Ms. Jones, how long have you known Marcus?"

"Five years," she looked shocked.

"Where did you meet?"

"Social Security Administration."

"Ms. Jones, isn't it true that you met Marcus while you were a stripper at a club?"

"No. Alexis actually met Marcus while SHE was a stripper in a club. Marcus and I have been friends since 1995 and we are now married. I am a teacher and have never been a stripper."

I stared at Alexis. Her leg was shaking. Her attorney started to ask about November 16, but the state's attorney stopped her. I wished I could have talked about it; I would have really lit into her.

"Ms. Jones, what happened at your last court appearance?" I told how Alexis stopped her car in front of us, provoking a fight, and then wrote another false report on me. The questions the defense attorney asked helped me more than hurt me. She was obviously looking for a different response. I was very strong and clear in what I was saying. I was determined not to let this bitch get away again.

"Ms. Jones, isn't it true that you are the one harassing Ms. Alexis?"

"No. I have no reason to harass Alexis. I have the man, the job, the house and the life Alexis desires. I have never called or visited Alexis' house. Alexis is deranged and cannot accept the fact that Marcus does not want to be with her. She lies and has made herself believe that she is me, when she is actually the real stalker. She needs to move on with her life and leave us alone."

The defense attorney looked at Alexis with disgust. She finally realized that Alexis had been lying to her all along. Alexis had a way of making people believe she was the victim. It was now Alexis' turn to get on the stand. I went to get Marcus and we sat down in the courtroom, waiting for her testimony.

The lawyer asked, "Ms. Mason, what happened the night on September 25, 2000?"

"It was raining and I was locked out of my house. Marcus was living with me and I needed to get the keys from him, so I went to LaKeacha's house. My newborn daughter was in the car and I wanted to get her out of the rain. When I knocked on the door, LaKeacha grabbed the bat from behind the door and tried to hit me with it. In the midst of trying to hit me, LaKeacha hit Marcus across the shoulder. I don't know why LaKeacha didn't bring her neighbor as a witness, because she saw the whole thing. And that's the truth, Your Honor."

Marcus and I sat there in awe. The people behind us were laughing saying, "She's lying." We couldn't believe she sat on the stand, under oath and told those bogus lies.

The state's attorney got up and said, "Ms. Mason, I have one question for you. Did you get your keys?"

Alexis looked like she had seen a ghost. Her mouth dropped open like she was about to speak, but no words came out.

The state's attorney asked again, "It's a simple yes or no answer, Ms. Mason. You left your newborn baby in the car while it was pouring down raining to get your keys from your live in boyfriend. You went through all of this trouble; did you get your keys?"

Her story fell apart right then. The defense attorney put her head down in shame. Alexis started rambling on about something and finally said, "No."

The judge said, "Ms. Mason. I don't believe your story. You had a baby three weeks prior, and this man was with another woman. You expect me to believe that you peacefully went to the other woman's house to get your keys. These two witnesses say that you had the bat, if anybody should have brought the neighbor to testify, it should have been you. I find you guilty of the charges of assault with a deadly weapon. I sentence you to one year jail time," A loud gasp was heard throughout the courtroom.

"Yes!" I yelped.

"Suspended, one year probation for each charge." *Damn* The judge continued. "That's two years of unsupervised probation. You will have no contact with Mr. or Mrs. Jett. You must stay at least 400 feet away from them. Furthermore, you will pay all court fees. If the Jett's called the police and say that you are near their house or job at anytime, you will be arrested, and you will serve two years in jail."

I was relieved. Although I was hoping for jail time, at least she didn't get away like she did with everything else. I looked over at her and she was crying with her head down. She should have been happy it was only probation, but she believed she was untouchable.

Now I had the power and control. If I saw her near my house or my job again, I would call and have her arrested. People started saying, "Now you should write a false report on her and have her black ass go to jail for real." I didn't feel like playing games. I just wanted my life back. I hoped this would be the end of her egregious acts.

I was still dealing with depression and panic attacks. As I was taking a bath at Tracy's house, I started crying uncontrollably and my body went into a shock. I couldn't move or talk. I couldn't get Marcus' attention. When he finally came to check on me, I was a mess. My hair was soak and wet. My face was twisted and my eyes were blood shot red. Marcus gave me a Paxil and held me until I fell asleep. When I woke up, I told Marcus I wanted to go home. The house was up for foreclosure, but I wanted to keep it.

We met with a housing counselor at St. Ambrose Housing Center. The counselor told us to file for Chapter 13 Bankruptcy, which would help us keep our house and put all of our bills on a payment plan. We were on cloud nine.

We called our attorney and told him what we wanted to do. He filed the papers. Marcus went to the house and painted, replaced the wallpaper and mowed the lawn. The house seemed so cold and distant. All of the utilities were off. Marcus got everything turned on again and got the house ready for us to move back in. We moved our bedroom from upstairs to downstairs and moved the boys' room upstairs, so we could hear what was going on around us.

On November 1, 2001, we moved home again. Our wedding was in one month, December 23, and it was time to make the final preparations. A few weeks later, I had breast reduction surgery to remove the damage done to my breasts. The damaged tissue would eventually cause problems, if it were not removed. This surgery changed my voluptuous DD cups to a proud C cup. The biggest scar that remained was a keloid in the shape of a big X right underneath my breast. Minor scars around my breast remained, but it was more cosmetic than medical, so I would have to wait until I could afford to have it removed.

Our finances were still messed up. We were hoping I would get the money from the car accident in time to pay for the wedding. The bankruptcy plan required us to pay the mortgage and all other bills on time each month. We had a mortgage, two car payments, car insurance payments, a gas and electric bill, child support payments and daily living expenses. In addition, we had to pay four hundred and twenty-five dollars a month on the bankruptcy plan and four hundred dollars a month for child support for Marcus' other two children. We weren't able to keep up with this much longer.

The money for the wedding was due on December 18th. We needed $3,000. We had zero. We tried to write a check to postpone paying, but they verified the account and saw the money wasn't in there. We either had to cancel the wedding or borrow the $3,000. By God's grace, we borrowed $3,000 in two days. Luckily, we had paid everyone else, but we missed the first bankruptcy payment and December's mortgage payment.

In planning for the wedding, I found relief from the day to day drama. Instead of the traditional wedding ceremony, we wanted our wedding party to walk down the aisle on our favorite love songs. We had the wedding rehearsal and dinner. Marcus had a bachelor party the night before, but my friends didn't give me a bridal shower. I was ok with relaxing at the spa, alone.

Saturday, December 23, 2001. Tracy and the girls came over to help me prepare for the wedding. Tracy was my maid of honor and my sisters and cousins were the bridesmaids. The wedding and reception were held at the elaborate, Martin East.

The dress I selected was a perfect rendition of a fairy tale princess dress. It featured stunning hand-beaded detail on the front and the sleeves. The full gathered skirt was gorgeously decorated with small pearls. The glass Cinderella shoes were a perfect match for the beautiful gown.

All invited guest were present and ready to witness the marriage of LaKeacha and Marcus. Security was in place, just in case something popped off. *Love* by Musiq SoulChild rang throughout the ceremony room, as the groomsmen walked down the aisle. When they reached halfway down the aisle, the bridesmaids joined them. The groomsmen reached over and kissed the bridesmaid's hand, and they both continued to the altar.

As Stevie Wonder's song, *You and I* began to play, it was my cue to walk down the aisle, escorted by my cousin LaShawn. The wedding was absolutely beautiful. I could not have imagined anything more special. Marcus was handsome in his tuxedo. We had the time of our life. We laughed and danced. Everybody ate, drank and was happy.

I looked at Marcus and thought he was worth everything I had gone through. I loved him so much. He wasn't violent and rough, like my family wanted him to be. He was so much more. He was compassionate and caring. I got mad at him sometimes, and I suspected he was involved with Alexis sometimes. That night, all I saw was my husband, my best friend.

Many of our guests didn't know we were married earlier that year. It didn't matter. This was a new beginning for us. Our love was unbreakable. After the wedding, we went home and slept peacefully. We were grateful God got us through another test.

CHAPTER 7:
THE END OF THE BEGINNING

"Now this is not the end. It is not even the beginning of the end. But it is, perhaps, the end of the beginning."
Winston Churchill

Slowly but surely, we began rebuilding our lives. We still had tons of debt, but we were working on paying everyone we owed. It was amazing how we survived all the drama of the last two years. Six months after the wedding, I was pregnant again.

I was happy, but I was still undergoing a lot of stress. My body and mind were not prepared for pregnancy and I had a miscarriage. My excitement was gone, another disappointing event in my life. I could sense this baby was another girl, so I named her, *Kellis Alliyah*. I was only four months when I miscarried, so there was no funeral, however, I still mourned her death.

It took me a while to do things by myself. I would not walk outside alone. I would not go to the mall alone. When walking from the school to my car, I always had someone with me. Every day, I thought, *This could be the day Alexis shoots me in the head.*

I decided to take out a $500,000 insurance policy on myself, declaring my mother the beneficiary. If I were killed, my kids would be taken care of. I also wrote my obituary and had my will prepared. I was preparing for death.

Finally, I decided *If I die, so be it. I cannot live my life in fear anymore.* I got rid of the gun. I stopped calling Marcus to open the door for me. I had a beautiful park in the back yard and never walked the park with my kids. So I made myself walk around the entire neighborhood alone, every evening. Dionte', Kaylah and I started going to the park.

Dionte' was in his last year of elementary school. He was oblivious to everything that happened. He loved to play sports, so we got him involved in basketball, baseball and football. Although very bright, Dionte' played more in school, than he worked. Trying to prepare him for middle school wasn't an easy task.

Kaylah was growing into a beautiful child. She was very smart and picked up on things easily. At 1 ½ years old, she was already prissy. She didn't like getting her clothes dirty, but she loved looking in the mirror and posing for the camera. Almost the spitting image of Marcus, Kaylah adored the grounds her daddy walked on. She was definitely a daddy's girl.

Marcus and I hoped to have another child, but after the miscarriage we decided to wait a little while. The following year, I conceived. This time, I was not as stressed out. I hoped for another little girl, but as long as I had a healthy baby, it didn't matter.

To further my education and career, my principal encouraged me to enroll in a leadership program at the College of Notre Dame to obtain my Master's Degree. He promised when I completed the program, I would have an assistant principal job; leading me to my dream of becoming a principal or having my own all girl's school. My principal and co-workers were still impressed with my teaching talents, along with my willingness to assist everyone, so he selected me to train several student teachers. In addition, I was appointed the fifth grade chairperson and was in charge of planning events and activities for the students, as well as, making the learning process challenging.

My goal was to make school exciting and fun for students. When my co-worker, Ms. Day asked me to help her start a girl's mentoring program, I said, "Yes!" Helping girls avoid becoming like Alexis Mason, was my mission and I was glad to take it head on.

To my surprise, I was voted Teacher of the Year in June 2003. I loved my co-workers, although they never knew the details of my two year ordeal with Alexis Mason, they helped me get through a lot of hard days. There was always a reason to laugh and smile at work. I guess it's true what they say; laughter is good for the soul.

A big baby shower was thrown in my backyard to celebrate the arrival of my new son, Kai Alexander. He was born on September 22. There was no drama or stress. Kai was 7 pounds and 13 ounces. Our family was complete. Marcus and I had no desire to have any more children. Between both of us, we had five. Marcus' son still came to visit each week, but Marcus had no relationship with his daughter.

After all that was done by her mother, I still encouraged him to pursue a relationship with his daughter. It may have been too early and she was too young at this point; but when she got older, I told him to try and build a relationship with her, despite her mother's actions. The child should not suffer because of her mother. In the meantime, I convinced him to send her gifts and toys throughout the years.

Things seemed to be going well for us. We saved our house. We caught up on all the bills. We started taking trips. We stopped talking about Alexis Mason and we were in love again, until Marcus started waking every morning, crying hysterically. What was happening now?

Marcus couldn't explain why he was crying. I took off of work and called every psychologist in the telephone book. Unfortunately all of the doctors were booked for weeks in advance. *Is everybody in Baltimore City crazy? What the hell is going on?*

Marcus started seeing a psychologist. He never invited me to his sessions and didn't discuss what happened, but his behavior changed towards me. He acted very distant and spent less and less time with me. He was always at a meeting or working longer hours.

He even changed his appearance. He wore gray or light brown contacts and made his hair extra curly. He wasn't as affectionate as he once was. He never wanted to cuddle like we used to and watch a movie(mainly something scary on the *Lifetime Channel)*. Instead, he was always out of the house or asleep when he was home.

In the last four years, Marcus and I had not spent a New Year's Eve out together. I convinced him to get a baby sitter and we stayed at the Renaissance Hotel in the Inner Harbor, for the New Year's Eve celebration. We ate dinner at *The Window* and watched fireworks from our table.

The next morning, Marcus left his cell phone in the bathroom. Being nosy, I looked through it. One number looked suspicious; it was named Hit-Em-Up Productions. His text to the person, *Happy New Year's Day!*

Knowing Marcus had been acting strange and this was an out of town number, I was curious to see who this person was. I wrote the number on a piece of paper and planned to look up the area code, when I was alone. When Marcus left the room to pick up some breakfast, I looked up the area code and called the number from the hotel room. A man answered. "Hello."

"Is this Hit Em Up Productions?" I asked shocked, expecting to hear a woman on the other end.

"No," he said hesitantly. A few minutes later, Marcus called asking why I was trying to destroy his surprise. He said the guy was handling a secret trip to Atlantic City he was planning for us on Valentine's Day. *How did the guy know it was me? Now you are texting travel agents to say Happy New Year early in the morning. Who does that?*

Marcus' continued with his new attitude. At that moment, he was certain being a husband and a father was too much. He told me he hadn't been out in four years, because he was always with me. He found a part-time security job and worked every weekend from 12 midnight to 12 noon. He left that job and went to his regular job, so I hardly saw Marcus on the weekends. We talked on the phone during the night, until a young lady started working with him, then the phone calls ended.

Still determined to improve my life, I joined Weight Watchers, acquired a membership to the YMCA and started line dancing class with my friend, Mo. In the last four years, I went from 140 pounds to 190 pounds, from a size 10 to a size 16. I didn't want to use the excuse of being pregnant three times in the last four years, forever, so I resolved to lose the extra weight and become sexy again.

My self-esteem was bruised and my finances were battered. I couldn't fit any of my stylish name brand clothing and I definitely couldn't afford to buy any new ones. My shoes were outdated, because I exchanged all my stilettos for teacher shoes with low heels. I changed my appearance to look like someone I never wanted to look like, a mother or a teacher.

No offense to either one, especially since I'm both, but I enjoyed being stylish. I wanted my kids to be proud to say, "That's my mama." Not because I dressed like a "hoochie mama", but because I was fashionable and dressed like a first lady. A lot of teachers wear low heals because it's comfortable, but that wasn't me. A lot of moms wear sweat suits or jeans with tennis, but that wasn't me either.

I always pride myself on being a great dresser, but over the years, all that changed. I dressed like I felt and I felt like I was in a dark place, so I wore big, dark clothing, never sexy, never stylish. My hair grew back nicely, but I continued wearing the wigs. Anything that could hide who I was, I wore.

Because of the stress and anxiety, I made up my mind to see a therapist. Before now, I never considered therapy for myself, since I believed it was only for mentally ill people. Nevertheless, I began seeing, Dr. Hilton, a thin white lady with short hair, once a week.

This lady cannot help me to overcome my issues. She doesn't understand what I went through as a black women and she definitely cannot relate to my situation.

To my surprise Dr. Hilton helped me to get my mental stability back on the right path. It was good to talk with someone who was not bias. She didn't know any of the parties involved, so she gave me her honest opinion and feedback. I freely talked about my past drama with Alexis and now my current drama with Marcus. Dr. Hilton asked me, "What about LaKeacha? What does LaKeacha want for herself?"

I never thought about it. It was always about Alexis, family, Marcus, babies, school and work, but it was never about LaKeacha. What did I want? At that moment, I only wanted peace, harmony and happiness. I couldn't remember what it felt like to be completely happy and stress free.

Although I was better, I always had to watch my surroundings. I was careful about who I befriended and what I said. I was a completely different person. I didn't have that upbeat, sassy, attitude I had before. I wasn't the tough girl that would cuss you out at the drop of a hat. I wasn't happy and bubbly anymore. Around people, I didn't talk much at all. I hid away and didn't want to be seen or heard. I didn't live. I just existed. I loved my kids and I loved my family, but I didn't know if I was a wife because it was the right thing to do, or because it was something I wanted to do.

One Sunday morning, Marcus woke up and fixed breakfast. He sat down on the bed and starting breathing hard.

I said, "What is it?"

He said, "I knew this would be hard, but not this hard," and handed me a letter.

Dear Keacha,

I am sorry for all the pain I have caused you, but I am not happy being here anymore. I can no longer look at you and know that I am constantly making you unhappy. I am not good enough for you. I don't deserve you. I cannot be the husband and father you want me to be. It is time for me to leave. I'm moving to live with my mother.
Marcus

I read the letter and said, "Okay." I was so hurt; I didn't know what else to say. I started crying and asked, "Can you leave now?"

Marcus packed all his things. I felt like a knife had stabbed me in the back. It hurt like hell to know that I'd been a fool for four years. Just to think I had been taking care of a man who didn't love me and didn't want our children, forced me to realize I'd been deceived and lied to.

I should have picked up the signs a long time ago. I should have known I was being used. I'd been busting my ass to be a good wife and mother. For what? To be told I was too good and he wasn't happy. It was his fault we weren't happy. He was the one who brought the crazy maniac baby mama into our lives; now he wanted to leave.

I was a wreck the entire day. Every time the phone rang, I told whoever called and started crying all over again. Clearly, I couldn't take care of the kids. Tracy came over to console me. I kept shedding tears and saying, "Marcus left me. After all this stuff I've been through, he left me."

Then my daughter started crying, "I want my daddy." I let her call him, so he could hear her bawling; then hung up the phone, without saying anything. Marcus had the audacity to call back and ask me if he could have the green Honda Accord. At this time, we had three cars, my Mitsubishi Gallant, a mini-van and a green Honda Accord. He wasn't getting either one. *If you want to leave, leave with the shit you brought, nigga.* Tracy stayed with me for a little while. After she left, I sobbed all night.

I gathered enough strength to call him. "What am I supposed to do now?" I didn't want him to come back home, but I felt he owed me some answers.

"I'm coming home. This was a mistake."

After Marcus returned home, things got worse. The way he treated me made my insides hurt. I guess he wanted me to see our relationship wasn't going to work, so I would break it off with him. It was clear this was the same game he played with Alexis. He avoided our house as much as possible. Throughout the week, he arrived home very late and ate dinner upstairs, staring at the television. Then he took sleeping pills to fall asleep.

His kisses were so cold and unloving. All of his clothes were packed at the top of the steps. I knew he had someone else. When he thought I was sleep, he laughed and talked on the phone. If I asked him who he was talking to, he'd say it was his cousin.

On the weekends that he didn't work, he visited his family's house and didn't invite me. He never called to see if we were okay. If I called him, he didn't answer the telephone. I ate dinner alone. I couldn't remember the last time we ate dinner together. As if the weekends weren't enough, he starting hanging out with his friends throughout the week; friends I never met. Marcus made sure to occupy all of his time with working and his new friends. He arrived home in the wee hours of the night and slept on the far side of the bed, curled up, as if he was praying I wouldn't touch him.

This was unusual for him and difficult for me to handle. It would have been different if this had always happened, but it never happened before. I refused to be married to a man who couldn't stand being around me. I needed to make some changes.

The last straw was when he was supposed to go out to the club with his best friend and didn't come home until the next afternoon. One side of me was worried. On the other hand, I knew he was playing games. I called his mother's house, but he wasn't there. I told his mother what was going on because I didn't know what Marcus was telling her. She listened, but she sounded like she really didn't care either. She said, "I will tell him to call you."

Afterwards, Marcus called and said, "I fell asleep over Jason's house. When I woke up, I went straight to work. I called your cell phone and left a message," he lied. I looked at my cell phone. He never called.

The following Saturday, I got so fed up with Marcus' behavior; I threw all of his clothes down the steps. I called him several times and left him a message saying that I had thrown all of his clothes into the street (to get his attention). He responded that he was getting off at 7:00 p.m., but came home around 4:00 the next morning. He slept on the floor all night. The next morning, he gave me another long speech.

"Keacha you don't understand. It makes me sad looking at you. When I'm around other people, I'm happy. When I'm here, around you and these kids, I'm sad. I'm tired of pretending that I want to be a husband, pretending that I like your family, and pretending that I am happy. I'm not happy and I am not pretending anymore!"

"Do you love me, Marcus?"

"Yes, I love you, but I'm not happy here."

"Do you still want to be with me?" I asked.

Marcus looked at me and wouldn't respond. I had my answer. Marcus did not want to be married anymore.

The next morning, I gave Marcus a taste of his own medicine. I wanted him to see how it felt to be stuck in the house with three kids all day. I got up and fixed myself up. I found the cutest outfit I had and left the house, without my cell phone. I didn't have anywhere to go, so I went to the grocery store and to the movies, alone.

As I was leaving the movies, I heard someone call me. "Lady." I hadn't been called that in a while, so I knew it had to be someone from my past. I turned around, it was Antoine. My heart started fluttering. I had not seen Antoine in five years. He had no idea what was going on in my life now. He was still fine as ever and still had that tough boy swag I loved. He grabbed me and hugged me closely.

"What's up, Ma?"

I was smiling from ear to ear. "Nothing much, how are you?"

"I'm good. Where have you been hiding for the last five years?"

"I haven't been hiding, just busy." At that moment I wish I could disappear. He was probably thinking, *Damn you big as hell*, so I kept looking down at the ground.

He picked up my hand and looked at my wedding ring. "You still married?"

Barely, I thought. "Yeah," I put on a fake smile.

"Happily?"

"What does that mean Antoine? All marriages have their ups and downs."

"Not if it were you and I."

"Excuse me; do you remember how you cheated on me?"

"She wasn't nobody, Ma. It was always about you. You came back to me after that."

"Yeah, but you wouldn't give up the street life."

"I have though. I have my own business. I own a couple of barbershops on this side of town and I have about five or six rental properties."

I smiled. "Look at you, you on the up and up now."

"Oh don't worry. I will still pop a nigga, but I'm trying to do the right thing now. I have a little girl."

"You do. What's her name?"

He took out a picture from his wallet. "Briana, but I call her Lil Lady."

I showed Antoine the family picture of Marcus and me, with our four kids (minus Alexis' daughter). We exchanged numbers and left. I was so embarrassed he saw me looking like a fat old lady. Although I was cuter than usual, I was not the same Lady he knew. I didn't know if he had heard about all the drama I went through, but I wasn't going to bring it up. I hoped and prayed he did not call me.

So many days I wanted to call Antoine and have him to put an end to all the nonsense, but I was married to Marcus and it didn't feel right. Marcus was supposed to protect me. I shouldn't have to call Antoine to take care of Marcus' problem, so I didn't call. Now Marcus was leaving me and I wasn't sure what was going to happen.

When I came home, the house was a mess. The kids were filthy and Marcus' clothes were neatly packed up. I told him that if he left this time, he wasn't coming back, ever. He stayed.

The following weekend, I gave my sister a birthday party. Usually, Marcus would be there, but this time, he was determined to stay away from my family. He arrived home about two in the morning. I told him that if I found out he was cheating on me, I would kill him. "Do you want to smell my dick?" was his response. I went to sleep.

The house had bad vibes. Nothing good was happening in that house. I tried to hold on to it, but it was unbearable. Marcus was diagnosed as depressed. Dionte' was having behavior problems in school. The babies were always sick. The bills were behind again. The Honda Accord was repossessed. The house was up for foreclosure, and I was seeing a therapist. It was too much on me.

I needed to get away. I needed to relocate. After researching the best places to live in the United States, I decided to move to Atlanta, Georgia. At that time, Atlanta was the third best place to live, right behind two cities in Florida.

I wasn't happy in Baltimore. I was tired of looking over my shoulder and not having complete peace of mind. I was tired of the bills and the bankruptcy notices. I was tired of my job and tired of taking care of everybody else, except me. I was almost finished my Master's Degree and it was time for a serious change. There was nothing negative about moving to Georgia, and nothing positive about staying in Baltimore.

When I first suggested moving to Atlanta, for a fresh start, Marcus was for it. Then, he changed his mind and said he was tired of going along with the plan. He was staying in Baltimore, would live with his mother and go back to school. I didn't care anymore. If Marcus wanted to stay in Baltimore, let him stay. I couldn't make Marcus happy; only God could help him. I had an uncle who lived in Atlanta for years, so he would help me, but I would be hours away from everyone else in my family. I prayed and prayed for the right decision. God told me to move to Atlanta. *If this is really God, then he will show me a sign.*

I put my house on the market on Monday, March 21, 2005. Ten days later, there was a contract on it for double what I paid for it. That was definitely a sign from God. About six weeks later, we went to settlement and prepared to move to Atlanta, Georgia.

I hoped Marcus would move to Atlanta and we could work on our marriage, but in my heart, I knew it was over between us. After selling my house, I got a check for $50,000. I resigned from my job, gave Marcus $10,000, paid the rent for the house in Atlanta for a year, paid off all my bills on the bankruptcy and moved my furniture and belongings to Atlanta. After all of that, I went on a second trip to Las Vegas with my family.

Following our return from Las Vegas, Marcus drove the babies and me to our new home in Atlanta. Dionte' stayed with his dad until the school year was over.

My mother cried. I cried. Everybody cried, but I knew it was the best for us. We arrived at our new home in Atlanta and Marcus decided he would transfer his job and live with us.

I was excited Marcus had made up his mind to fight for his marriage and make it work. In Atlanta, we could start fresh and have the life we had always dreamed of. The home we rented was already twice the size of our previous home in Baltimore. We had a bigger fenced in yard so the kids could run and play all day. The neighborhood was very nice.

Atlanta had a completely different vibe from Baltimore. The people here seemed to want something better out of their lives. Everything was big in Atlanta. All the houses seemed big. All the cars seem to be luxury cars. Even the churches were the biggest churches I had ever seen.

One month later, I had another scare of my life. I signed Kaylah up for summer camp at one of the nearby schools and put Kai in a daycare so I could find a job. My period was extremely heavy and I didn't feel well. I called Marcus and said, "I'm bleeding large blood clots and going to the bathroom every 30 minutes or less to change. Something's not right. I'm going to order a pizza and lay down for a little while."

When the pizza man arrived, I opened the door. Boom! I passed out and hit the ground. A few moments later I gained consciousness. The pizza man was very helpful, but I urged him not to call 911. I told him I would be fine.

I managed to drive to the camp to pick up Kaylah. In the ten minutes it took me to arrive at the school, my seat was completely soiled in blood. I got lightheaded and started throwing up. The counselors called 911. By the time, the ambulance arrived, I could not breathe. I was in and out of consciousness, until I passed out and was rushed to Southern Regional Hospital. The camp called my uncle to pick up Kaylah and retrieve Kai from the daycare.

Upon arrival at the hospital, my blood count was .4. I was diagnosed with fibrocystic disease and had to get a blood transfusion, immediately. I stayed in the hospital a few days and was scheduled to have a hysterectomy in the upcoming weeks, to prevent this episode from happening again.

My mom called Marcus and asked him to drive her to Atlanta. Although I was sick and needed him, Marcus was not happy about coming to Atlanta. He was very cold and distant towards me. When it was time for them to return to Baltimore, Kaylah was crying hysterically, as we stood in front of the house. Marcus jumped in the car and drove off. I was appalled at his behavior.

Taking six weeks to recuperate from the hysterectomy as the doctor suggested, was impossible, I needed to find a job. The money I got from the settlement was slowly disappearing. I applied and interviewed for several teaching positions at schools close to my house. I was trained to be an assistant principal. However, most school districts preferred newcomers to start as teachers, and move their way up to a leadership position. So I was starting over, with a $20,000 salary cut. Fortunately, I was hired at a school, ten minutes away from my house, as a fifth grade teacher.

On the bright side, I had a fresh new beginning and left my past behind. However, I was in a new place, with absolutely no friends. I quickly learned about people in the "Bible Belt". It was unusual for me to hear so many people talk about the Bible and church at work, yet the same people would talk about people and crucify others with their tongue. In Baltimore, nobody talked about church at work. We didn't have Bible Study after school. We didn't meet at each other's houses for prayer. Atlanta was definitely different. I was careful to make friends with other people, whom I thought were genuine.

In spite of the phony Christians I'd encountered at work, I joined a church, Believe Faith Ministries International. Joining this church was the best thing for me. The pastor taught about overcoming struggles and getting the best that God had for me.

This church was different from any church I had experienced. People seemed free. There was no dress code. The music was loud. They had flashing lights across the stage and the preacher made you feel like you were supposed to be rich and debt free. He taught that you were an heir to the kingdom. I knew I had something on the inside of me, but I didn't know God was like this. The God this preacher spoke of was a comforter and a father. Both of which I needed right now.

Marcus' attitude had not changed towards me. He continued to be cordial, but he was making plans to live his life without me. Marcus was responsible for making the payments on the van. To my surprise, the loan was in default. I received a call indicating the van would be picked up. Apparently, Marcus had taken the $10,000 that I had given him, made a down payment on another vehicle and stopped paying the note on the van altogether. I immediately agreed they could come and get the van. I refused to pick up the slack for anything else pertaining to Marcus.

When Marcus moved to Atlanta in October, he sat in front of the TV all evening and wouldn't say a word. We needed to talk, so one of my new friends, Zee agreed to watch the kids for us. Marcus and I went to dinner at Johnny Carrinos.

"So what's going on I asked?"

Marcus signed, "I don't want to be married anymore."

"That's it. That's why you walking around here all depressed. Do you want to see a counselor first?"

"No. I am sure about what I want. I want to be happy."

"Ok, Marcus, Let's get a divorce."

With my inside falling to pieces, I held my composure and ate my dinner. I knew it was over a long time ago, but I continued to hold on, thinking Marcus would change his mind and come back to build the marriage that we were supposed to have. Marcus wasn't interested in rebuilding our marriage. He wouldn't even consider talking to a counselor. This time I was letting go of the relationship and never looking back.

I would not take responsibility for Marcus being unhappy, just for the sake of staying married. I couldn't imagine living in a house for years, with Marcus' depression and unhappiness. He deserved to be happy, just as much as I did and I would not stand in the way any longer. Yes, I was hurt and distraught. For the last five years, I depended on Marcus to take care of me and now I was on my own, just me, my kids and God.

To make things worse, Marcus suggested he could live upstairs in the guest room and I would stay downstairs in the master's suite. *Are you fucking kidding me?* I told him that wasn't happening and he needed to move out by December 31.

After all of that, I still gave Marcus a year to decide if he wanted us to stay married. Marcus moved out on New Year's Eve, 2005. I went to church. I was hurting and cried during the entire service. Crying seemed to be the thing I did most and best. Where was God? Why wouldn't this pain end?

I felt like a failure. I was stalked, beaten and abused because of a man who eventually left me anyway. Now I was a single mom with three children. I was embarrassed, stripped to nothing. This was like being burned and tortured, all over again.

I was angry with myself, angry with Marcus, angry with Alexis and especially angry with God. Why did he make me promise not to kill Alexis all those years ago? Why did he let her get away with everything she did? Now she could gloat in the fact that Marcus and I were divorcing. Did God get pleasure out of watching me get hurt and abused? What did I do to deserve all of the heartache and torture I was receiving? Why wouldn't God allow me to have peace and happiness? What about the loving God the preacher talked about? Couldn't he stop the devil from harassing me? Couldn't he say to the devil, "That's enough, she has endured enough!"

CHAPTER 8:
OVERCOME EGREGIOUS ACTS

"We must develop and maintain the capacity to forgive. He who is devoid of the power to forgive is devoid of the power to love."
Dr. Martin Luther King, Jr.

After divorcing Marcus, trials and tribulations continued. Divorce actually felt like death. I had lost another friend, just like I lost my sister, my friend Kim, and my baby girl; I lost Marcus. I experienced profound disappointment, grief, stress and depression. Dionte' was attending a school in Atlanta and had an ongoing behavior problem. Kaylah cried non-stop for her dad. She loved her dad more than anybody in the world. Kai, on the other hand, was too young to understand what was happening.

Marcus began picking the kids up less and less until it became non-existent. Over the years, I tried to keep a friendship with Marcus, but soon realized that we could not be friends. We were amiable for the kid's sake, but I needed to move forward in my life and become successful. More than anything, I wanted to have a life enriched with peace and happiness. I couldn't remember the last time I could say that I was truly happy.

I started learning about forgiveness. The Bible says to forgive others because God has forgiven you. People say forgive, but never forget. I learned that forgiveness is a decision to let go of resentment and thoughts of revenge. I also learned people who forgive are happier and healthier, than those who don't. Lastly, people who are taught how to forgive become less angry, feel less hurt, are more optimistic, are more compassionate, have more confidence and are more forgiving in other situations. I still had many questions about forgiveness.

Yes, I wanted to have a sense of integrity, peace, happiness and an overall well being. But how could I forgive someone who had nearly destroyed my life? How was I supposed to forgive? How could I forgive someone who didn't admit that he or she was wrong? How could I forgive, but not forget? Could forgiveness really help me become a better person? Did forgiveness really matter? How could I forget that I was walked out on and left alone in a state that was miles away from my family? How was I supposed to forgive all of the things that I endured?

I also heard forgiving someone means you are saying you trust them again to have them in your life. There was no way I would ever trust Alexis Mason, not in my life, especially not around my children. I also had a hard time trusting Marcus. He became a person, I didn't know anymore.

Every day, I looked in the mirror at the scars of that night. No matter how many times I put it out of my head. There was no hiding what I saw in the mirror and no suppressing untrusting feelings I

had towards people. I couldn't piece together the broken marriage I lost or bring back the baby I miscarried. There was no way I could erase the experiences I endured because of Alexis Mason. So I prayed and asked God to teach me how to forgive. He told me to write a letter. So I wrote...
Dear Alexis,

On November 16, 2000, someone came into my home, brutally attacked me and burned me with chemicals. Although you continue to deny that it was you, we both know who it was. It's sad how a young lady would go to such extremes to hurt someone and try to kill an unborn child. You called my house. You came to my house. You destroyed my life. Why? Because you wanted Marcus? Really? No, you suffer from low self-esteem. You don't love yourself and you felt that I had something you did not have or could not have.

You don't know what I have been through to get the success that I had until you came along. Not that you care, but let me enlighten you. I was molested by my cousin when I was a young girl. My sister died from leukemia when I was 12-years old and I was a teenage mom at 17. I've had my share of challenges. I struggled day in and day out to finish high school, go to college and get a teaching job at a wonderful school. Then you came along to destroy it all.

Did you think Marcus would be with you after burning me? Did you think if my face was burned beyond recognition, as you wrote, he would no longer love me? The love that Marcus and I shared as friends happened way before you appeared.

I pray that your two daughters do not adopt your behaviors. I pray that you find the love that you so desperately need and seek medical attention. I know that you are wondering why I didn't seek revenge on all the things that you have done. Although it was hard, I made the decision to let God deal with you. Without a doubt, I know that whatever seeds you've planted will come back to you. You will suffer beyond what I suffered. You will live a sad and miserable life, beyond what I experienced unless you get right with God. Of all the things you've done to break me, I still survived. What you did for evil, God used for his good, so I forgive you!
Keacha

To my surprise, I felt a burden lifted off of me. I felt peace that I didn't have before. Although I didn't send her the letter, I felt like I was free…free from all of the things that had held me back for so long. I felt like shackles were actually broken from my life.

I wasn't the victim anymore because I asked God to relinquish the power and control she had over my life through forgiveness. I realized I had to forgive Alexis. In actuality, she was the victim of low self-esteem and mental instability. I actually had understanding, empathy and compassion for her. I learned it wasn't her, but the evil spirit had overtaken her and caused her to do the things she did. This spirit was sent from hell to destroy me and keep me off the path of greatness God has for me. Alexis was a vessel being used by Satan to complete his mission. I don't deny responsibility in what she did or justify her wrongdoing. However, I needed the peace of true forgiveness to move on with my life.

The next person I needed to forgive was Marcus. It was more difficult to forgive Marcus. After all of the drama I endured because of him and all of the things we had gone through, in the end, he still left me. He walked away from the marriage and from the friendship. I was hurt because I loved and trusted him. I felt angry, sad and confused. I didn't think I could forgive him so easily. Alexis had a mental problem, but what was Marcus' excuse? Nevertheless, I knew that forgiveness was the only way for me to move forward. So I wrote…

Dear Marcus,

In 1995, we would never have imagined that we would end up divorced and angry, ten years later. We never anticipated us not being best friends. We never thought that we would endure all of the heartbreaks that we have encountered. All marriages have their ups and downs, but we started on downs and never seemed to make it up. I loved you. I have said some things and have done some things to make you think otherwise, but you were my best friend.

A lot of times I questioned your role in the whole incident with Alexis. I was uncertain about some of your actions and I wondered if you had anything to do with that night. I often made excuses for you because in my heart, I didn't believe you knew Alexis were going to attack me on that night. However, as my husband, you did not protect me like you should have. You did not stand up to Alexis in my defense. In many ways, you protected Alexis from getting killed by my family because you wouldn't give them her information.

More than anything, I am hurt that you would leave me alone in Atlanta and treat me so badly after all that we have been through. We were supposed to stay together through thick and thin, but that's obsolete now. No matter what, we cannot deny that fact that we have beautiful children together. I pray that we can be the best parents for them, despite being divorced. I forgive you for all that you have done to me and I ask for forgiveness for all that I have done to you. I wish the absolute best for you.
Keacha

Last but not least, I needed to ask God to forgive me. I did not provoke some of the incidents that happened to me, but I am far from perfect, and I have had my share of wrongdoings. So I wrote a letter to God.

Dear God,

It's me, Keacha. Please forgive me for all the transgressions I have done in my life. Forgive me, Lord, for not treating others the way that you require me to treat them. Forgive me for confusing being proud with being prideful. I know that pride is one of the worst sins. Forgive me, Lord, for not representing you in everything I do.

God, please teach me how to forgive myself. So many days I wish I had not reunited Marcus. So many days I wish that I had not opened that door for the guy. So many days I blame myself for the things that I have endured. Thank you for your forgiveness. In Jesus' name. Amen.
Keacha

After my heartfelt prayers and letters, I began to seek God for what he wanted me to do in my life. I thought to myself, *Everything happens for a reason. So what was the reason I experienced molestation, endured the death of a sister, became a teenage mom, encountered stalking, being brutally attacked and burned while pregnant, survived the impact of a car and suffered: a miscarriage, bankruptcy, foreclosure, repossession, anxiety attacks, blood transfusion and divorce?*

I concluded most of what I experienced was issues related to women and girls. I thought about Social Butterflies, the group I started with my co-worker before I left Baltimore. *That's it! It's my mission to work with women and girls. But how?* I was too embarrassed to tell anyone about all of the things I had endured. I didn't want my family to find out most of the tragedies. Besides, I was a failure. How could I possibly help someone else become successful, if I wasn't successful?

The best revenge is success. Become successful by creating the life you want to live. Use your experiences to help girls and women live better lives.

Becoming successful was not an easy task. Statistics for me to fail were greater than my chances of success. I didn't want to fall into other people's plan of failure for my life, so I designed my own life's plan. I changed my poor thinking, neglectful behaviors, poor habits and poor choices and transformed my thinking, so it would be in direct alignment to the Word of God. I made a choice to be successful, in spite of all the drama I endured. I started by creating a positive vision of my future, developing a plan to get there, communicating the plan and working the plan until it came to pass.

The idea of change made me uncomfortable, but it was my responsibility to make better choices for myself and for my children. I chose to further my education instead of overindulging in entertainment, so I enrolled in a specialist program in 2006, taking one class at a time. Eventually, I graduated with a Specialist Degree in 2010.

I chose to work instead of resting. With the help of my former co-worker and her fiancé, we established Social Butterflies, Inc. as a non-profit organization in 2007, establishing chapters throughout Atlanta, Baltimore and other urban cities.

I chose to accept the truth that I can be successful, instead of believing the delusional lies labeling me a failure. I chose confidence over doubt. I chose to change my attitude from a negative attitude to a more positive, optimistic attitude.

My attitude determined my altitude. I stopped allowing others to control my attitude. I had become hostile, angry, untrusting and bitter, so I had to replace those behaviors with peace, joy, love and patience.

I studied people who were successful, that I admired and respected, whose behavior I could model. There were many people who experienced worse trauma, disappointments, despair and heartache, yet they were successful. I studied and learned about those people by reading inspirational books such as:

1. *The Holy Bible*
2. *Twelve Pillars* by Jim Rohn and Chris Widener
3. *Live Your Best Life Now* by Joel Osteen
4. *The Purpose Driven Life* by Rick Warren
5. *Who Moved My Cheese?* by Spencer Johnson, M.D.
6. *The Great Investment: Faith, Family and Finance* by Bishop T.D. Jakes
7. *The Secret* and *The Power* by Rhonda Byrne
8. *Seven Habits of Highly Successful People* by Stephen R. Covey
9. *Think and Grow Rich* by Napoleon Hill
10. *Do You! 12 Laws to Access the Power in You to Achieve Happiness and Success* by Russell Simmons
11. *A Piece of Cake* by Cupcake Brown
12. *Success, Ebony and Essence Magazines*
13. *8 Steps to Creating the Life You Want: The Anatomy of a Successful Life* by Creflo A. Dollar
14. *Total Life Prosperity* by Creflo A. Dollar
15. *Praying God's Will for Your Life* by Stormie Omartian

From these readings, I learned that success comes when you develop yourself beyond your current situation. You have to work harder on yourself than you work on your job. That's exactly what I did. After receiving my Specialist Degree, I continued in a doctorate program to increase my education.

I was determined to get the best education possible. I enlarged my vision by thinking about what I really wanted in life by looking through the eyes of faith. I knew that God would not take me through all the trials and tribulations, if he did not have something better for me.

The image I held on the inside of my life was what I wanted to live on the outside. This image became a part of my life, my thoughts, conversations and actions. I created a vision board, a visualization tool that is used to activate the universal law of attraction. My vision board included goals and dreams, supported by biblical scriptures. Each day I witnessed my goals and dreams becoming a reality, through my eyes of faith and hard work.

I also changed the people whom I was associating and surrounded myself with the best people or the people who had my best interest. I learned from Jim Rohn and Chris Widener that there are three categories in which I should place people: disassociation, limited association and expanded association.

I dissociated myself with people who had negative attitudes, accepted failures, and lived a life of mediocrity. I limited association with people who did not have their own dreams and visions. I expanded association with winners and successful people who had their own dreams and visions and who support my dreams. I surrounded myself with people who had positive attitudes and optimism.

Through my revelations, I concluded that life will follow my expectations so I developed my own personal philosophy: *Think Greatness. Expect Greatness. Live Greatness.* To think greatness simply means life will follow your expectations; therefore, think as great as you can think. *I am what I think I am! If I think I am great, then I will be.*

I expect greatness to follow me everywhere I go and expect greatness displayed in everything I do. It was difficult to accept this profound knowledge because I was told so many times, "You think you're all that." or "You always have to outdo everybody else." So I tried to limit my abilities. I tried to do what normal people did. Then I realized I can't help expecting greatness. I can't change the way I think and become mediocre because someone else is uncomfortable with my expectations. My expectation of excellence was different from other people's definition of excellence, and that was perfectly fine. However, I needed to "do me".

Everyone has his or her own mission on Earth. My mission is to do something great by helping others. Why should I allow other people who are not satisfied with their own lives to hinder me from doing what God wants me to do?

In the beginning, I got offended when my friends didn't support me or wasn't excited about a new project, I was involved in. Finally, I learned how to take people as a grain of salt and continued to follow what God required of me. There are always going to be haters, even among family and friends. As long as God was on my side, I kept it moving.

Lastly, I decided to live greatness. As a daughter of the Most High, I should live with greatness. I should live in peace and harmony, with the love of God. I should live in the best house, drive the best car and have the best job.

Rebuilding my self-image was a never-ending process. I learned from the Bible that I was made in the image of God. *If I'm made in the image of God; God is a king and I am the daughter of a king, I should live and act like the daughter of a king.* From that point, I did not seek the approval of others, only the approval of God. I lived and conformed by behavior, like the daughter of a king. I built my self-esteem by reading certain passages and creating my own *21 Rules of Success*, which I recited and read each day until they were instilled in my heart and mind.

21 Rules of Success

1. **Always be thankful and praise God for everything.**
   Hebrews 13:15 By him therefore let us offer the sacrifice of praise to God continually, that is, the fruit of our lips giving thanks to his name.
2. **Never complain.**
   Philippians 2:14 Do everything without complaining or arguing.
3. **Everything I do is for God's glory.**
   1 Corinthians 2:7 Now, we speak of God's secret wisdom, a wisdom that has been hidden and that God destined for our glory before time began.
4. **Take off all timelines. Let God lead the way.**
   Deuteronomy 28:13 The LORD will make you the head, not the tail. If you pay attention to the commands of the LORD your God that I give you this day and carefully follow them, you will always be at the top, never at the bottom.
5. **Keep my eyes on the promises of God for my life. God wants me to have good success.**
   Joshua 1:7 Be strong and very courageous. Be careful to obey all the law my servant Moses gave you; do not turn from it to the right or to the left, that you may be successful wherever you go.
   Joshua 1:8 Do not let this book of the law depart from your mouth; meditate on it day and night, so that you may be careful to do everything written in it. Then you will be prosperous and successful.
6. **If it doesn't fit, don't force it!**
   Hebrews 11:40 God had planned something better for us so that only together with us would they be made perfect.
7. **Never look back. Let go of the past!**
   Genesis 19:26 But Lot's wife looked back, and she became a pillar of salt.

Hebrews 11:26 He regarded disgrace for the sake of Christ as of greater value than the treasures of Egypt, because he was looking ahead to his reward.

8. **Keep the faith. Be faithful to God. Put action to my faith and do good deeds for others.**
   Matthew 9:29 Then he touched their eyes and said, "According to your faith will it be done to you."
   Matthew 15:28 Then Jesus answered, "Woman, you have great faith! Your request is granted." And her daughter was healed from that very hour.
   Matthew 17:20 He replied, "Because you have so little faith. I tell you the truth, if you have faith as small as a mustard seed, you can say to this mountain, 'Move from here to there' and it will move. Nothing will be impossible for you."

9. **NO and CAN'T are unacceptable! Be strong and very courageous. I can do all things through Christ who strengthens me.**
   Matthew 19:26 Jesus looked at them and said, "With man this is impossible, but with God all things are possible."
   Philippians 4:13 I can do all things through Christ which strengthen me.

10. **Be a good steward over what God has given me. Save money and invest in good things. Do not overspend unnecessarily.**
    Luke 12:42 And the Lord said, "Who then is that faithful and wise steward, whom his Lord shall make ruler over his household, to give them their portion of meat in due season?"
    Matthew 25:27 Thou oughtest therefore to have put my money to the exchangers, and then at my coming I should have received mine own with usury.

11. **Give tithes and a freewill offering. Pay all debts and responsibilities.**

Malachi 3:10 Bring ye all the tithes into the storehouse, that there may be meat in mine house, and prove me now herewith, saith the LORD of hosts, if I will not open you the windows of heaven, and pour you out a blessing, that there shall not be room enough to receive it.

Luke 18:12 I fast twice in the week, I give tithes of all that I possess.

2 Kings 4:7 Then she came and told the man of God. And he said, Go, sell the oil, and pay thy debt, and live thou and thy children of the rest.

12. **Love God and your neighbors. Treat others as you wish to be treated regardless of the situation. Be a blessing to others.**

Deuteronomy 30:16 In that I command thee this day to love the LORD thy God, to walk in his ways, and to keep his commandments and his statutes and his judgments, that thou mayest live and multiply: and the LORD thy God shall bless thee in the land whither thou goest to possess it.

Matthew 5:44 But I say unto you, Love your enemies, bless them that curse you, do good to them that hate you, and pray for them which despitefully use you, and persecute you.

13. **Do not worry or stress. Worrying is an insult to God. God will supply ALL of my needs. He will help me, because he watches over me.**

Matthew 6:25 Therefore I tell you, do not worry about your life, what you will eat or drink; or about your body, what you will wear. Is not life more important than food, and the body more important than clothes?

Matthew 6:34 Therefore do not worry about tomorrow, for tomorrow will worry about itself. Each day has enough trouble of its own.

14. **Know that my purpose in life is to worship God in all I do. I was created for his glory. My mission on earth is to inspire and motivate people to be more like Jesus. I am not here for my own purpose and mission, but for God's glory.**
    Exodus 23:25 Worship the LORD your God, and his blessing will be on your food and water. I will take away sickness from among you.
    Revelation 15:4 Who will not fear you, O Lord, and bring glory to your name? For you alone are holy. All nations will come and worship before you, for your righteous acts have been revealed.
15. **Seek FIRST the kingdom of heaven. God gave me the keys, so use them and don't lose them.**
    Matthew 6:33 But seek first his kingdom and his righteousness, and all these things will be given to you as well.
    Matthew 16:19 I will give you the keys of the kingdom of heaven; whatever you bind on earth will be bound in heaven, and whatever you loose on earth will be loosed in heaven."
16. **Fast and pray. Ask God about everything, and for everything and I will receive it. Make sure I am doing what God wants me to do, not what I want to do. Listen for God to speak to my heart and read the Bible to hear from God. God will answer my prayers. WAIT for his response.**
    Matthew 7:7 Ask and it will be given to you; seek and you will find; knock and the door will be opened to you.
    Psalm 66:20 Praise be to God, who has not rejected my prayer or withheld his love from me!
17. **Speak good things into existence. Write my vision and goals and make them plain.**
    Proverbs 6:2 Thou art snared with the words of thy mouth, thou art taken with the words of thy mouth.

Proverbs 8:6 Hear; for I will speak of excellent things; and the opening of my lips shall be right things.

Habakkuk 2:2 And the LORD answered me, and said, Write the vision, and make it plain upon tables, that he may run that readeth it.

18. **God owes me nothing. I owe him all the praises.**

    1 Chronicles 16:25 For great is the LORD, and greatly to be praised: he also is to be feared above all gods.

19. **Choose cosmos over chaos.**

    Deuteronomy 30:19 I call heaven and earth to record this day against you, that I have set before you life and death, blessing and cursing: therefore choose life, that both thou and thy seed may live.

20. **Be a living sacrifice.**

    Romans 12:1 I beseech you therefore, brethren, by the mercies of God, that ye present your bodies a living sacrifice, holy, acceptable unto God, which is your reasonable service.

21. **Brings others to Christ by living a true godly life and being an example of how a child of God should live.**

    Matthew 28:18-20 And Jesus came and spake unto them, saying, All power is given unto me in heaven and in earth. Go ye therefore, and teach all nations, baptizing them in the name of the Father, and of the Son, and of the Holy Ghost. Teaching them to observe all things whatsoever I have commanded you: and, lo, I am with you always, even unto the end of the world. Amen.

CHAPTER 9:
EVERYTHING HAPPENS FOR A REASON

"Opposition is a natural part of life. Just as we develop our physical muscles through overcoming opposition-such as lifting weights-we develop our character muscles by overcoming challenges and adversity."
Stephen R. Convey

Present Day

"Keacha, guess who I saw in the village?" my sister Angie asked.

"Who?"

"Antoine!"

"OMG, for real!"

"He still looks the same. He asked about you. I told him that you lived in Atlanta now, but you were here for the holidays. He gave me his number to give to you, but I told him he could stop by here anytime."

"You did what? OMG let me get dressed, just in case he comes over."

So much had happened in my life since I last saw Antoine. I was so embarrassed; I could hardly hold my head up, five years ago. I can't believe it's been eleven years since Alexis Mason attempted to ruin my life and five years since Marcus walked out on me. It's amazing the transformations a person goes through as an adult.

At this point in time, I am perfectly confident in who I am and who I'm supposed to be. I'm back to my old self, without the profanity and popping off on people. Although I have to bring it out sometimes with a few folks who have to test me.

Over the years, I've learned that people will judge you for your appearance and what they see, instead of getting to know you. The main people who say only God can judge, are the ones placing judgments.

Nobody knows what a person goes through to make them the person they are. All of our life experiences shape us to be the person that others see, whether good, bad or ugly. It saddens me when people don't let go of the past and walk around bitter and angry, instead of moving on with their lives, so they could enjoy what God has for them.

DING DONG! The door bell rings. I knew it was Antoine, but I wanted to make sure I made a grand entrance, so I let Angie open the door. "Keacha! Antoine is here."

I walked down the stairs wearing my dark denim PZI skinny jeans, a matching logo t-shirt, and my patent leather Christian Louboutin red bottoms, 4 inch heels. Yep, I was back and in full effect. I had lost a little weight, but I wore my curves proudly. Over the years, the weight gain caused my breast to grow back to their normal size; it seemed as if the breast reduction never happened. I was fine with that as well.

Antoine had the biggest grin on his face. He probably was thinking, *Why the hell does this girl have on heels in the house?* I was making a statement.

After a long embrace, Antoine and I cuddled on the chair and started talking. "You are lookin' good Ma."

"Thank you. You are looking quite handsome yourself."

"What have you been up to? Fill me in on the last 10 years since you walked out of my life."

"Where should I start?"

"Wherever you want. I'm all yours."

"Well the kids are big now. Kaylah is eleven. She is one of the smartest girls in her school. She sings, she dances and she is an excellent artist. She's also plays the flute and wants to play the piano. She's multi-talented. My baby, Kai, is 8 years old. He loves to draw and he loves legos. Kai is much like me. He's quiet and stays to himself, but he does not hold his tongue for anyone. He acts like a lil old man sometimes. You remember Dionte'. He just turned nineteen."

Just then Dionte' walked up the stairs from the basement. "Here he is." Dionte' and Antoine clapped hands.

"You remember me man? I used to keep you with me all the time. You're a grown man now. What are you doing with yourself?"

"I'm finishing high school and I'm going to culinary arts school afterwards. I also write and perform music on the side. I wrote a song for mommy's book."

"That's great. Keep up the good work son." Antoine turned to me. "Are you sure that's not my son?"

"I'm sure." I laughed.

"How is your sister? I see the big belly."

"Yeah, she is expecting another son in February. She has been doing good for herself."

"What about those feisty girls you used to hang out with?"

"Tracy, Anecia and Shawna. Tracy is in a relationship and has a beautiful little girl. She works as a big time cooperate professional in Washington, DC. Shawna has two little girls. She is a reading coordinator for Baltimore City Public Schools. Anecia is married, with a little girl and works at the post office. Everybody is doing well."

"What about you?"

"Me. I'm doing good. I still teach. I'm teaching fourth grade this year. I established a non-profit organization for girls and I'm finishing my doctorate degree. Are you on Facebook?"

"No," he said. I showed Antoine my Facebook page.

"Damn, you've been living it up in Atlanta." I told Antoine about my new house, all of the trips I have taken in the last five years and all of the celebrities I've had the pleasure of meeting.

"So what about this book Dionte' said he wrote a song for?" I handed Antoine a draft of Egregious Acts. He read the back cover.

"Is this true?"

"Yes."

"Tell me about it."

"Are you sure you want to hear all of that?"

"Yes," he said. I told Antoine the entire saga of Alexis and Marcus.

"So let me get this straight. Was all of this going on when I saw you a few years back?"

"Yes."

"And you didn't mention it?"

"I was embarrassed. I didn't want you to know." His eyes displayed disappointment.

"What happened to the promise we made to call each other if we ever needed anything?"

"But I was married to Marcus. I couldn't call you to fix his problems."

"Was Marcus burned or were you burned?"

"Me." I looked down. Antoine always knew how to check me. "It's ok now. Everything happens for a reason."

"Really. What's the reason?"

"I work with girls now. I have programs all around the country, teaching girls how to become better women."

"So, this Alexis Mason, is she still alive?"

"Yeah, she said you two were good friends."

"What! I don't know an Alexis Mason."

"Tall, dark-skinned, she used to be a stripper and drove a lil black car."

"I have no recollection of her."

"Anyway, I heard she owns a hair salon, had another child and lives somewhere in Harford County. When I first got my *Facebook* page, I received an anonymous message that read, "You are a fake bitch!" When I responded, the person wrote, "Sound like you got venom in your voice." Last year, I drove my new car to Baltimore for Thanksgiving. It was parked right outside my mother's house, and someone wrote a gigantic capital A on the hood."

"Give me her name and address."

"How do you know I have that information?"

"I trained you Ma, I know you have it." I wrote the information on a piece of paper.

"What is Marcus punk ass doing now? Is he still in Atlanta?"

"No. He moved back here last year."

"So let me get this straight. After all of this you went through with this crazy chick, he left you in Atlanta with the kids."

"Yes. It's cool, Antoine. I'm good."

"No, it's not cool, Ma. He should have handled this. He should have protected you. What kind of nigga let some "hoe" destroy his family and let her ass live? You should have called me or came by the house. My grandmother has lived in the same house for the last thirty years. This would have never happened if you had stayed with me."

"I know. What are you going to do?"

"Luckily, Marcus is your children's father or I would blow that muthafucka away. When you get back to Atlanta, I'll have my friend, Buck, take you to buy a gun and go with you to the gun range to practice. In Georgia, you can carry a gun with a license, so complete your application when you get home."

He counts out six one hundred dollar bills and hands them to me. "This should cover the purchase of a gun. Alexis. Don't worry about her. I promise she won't be a threat any longer. And you know…"

"…you don't make empty promises or idle threats." I finished the sentence. Antoine stayed into the wee hours of the night. All I could think about was Mary J. song, Mr. Wrong… *Bad boys ain't no good. Good boys aint no fun. Lord knows that I should, run off with the right one…*

Although he still had connections to the hood, Antoine had changed his life around. He had been married and now divorced. His youngest daughter was eleven and he was ready for a change, away from Baltimore. This time I was keeping my bad boy.

CHAPTER 10: MY ADVICE

Today, I am living a life that I would not have thought possible 10 years ago. I realize my life experiences have prepared me to complete the mission God has for me, which is to inspire, motivate and encourage girls and women to reach success. I now enjoy a life of peace and happiness with my three beautiful children. However, I would like to share information with you I wish I had known, to prevent a lot of the heartaches I experienced.

Although my life was no movie, movies such as *Fatal Attraction, The Crush, Single White Female* and most recently, *Obsessed featuring Beyonce,* portray female psychopath stalkers as Caucasian, heterosexual, single women in their mid 30s. Contrary to popular belief, African-American females also have tendencies to become stalkers. Stalking is the willful, malicious, and repeated following and harassing of another person that threatens his or her safety.

Women are more likely than men to engage in same-sex stalking and tend to pursue their victims for one to five years. In my case, I was stalked for two years. Stalking is progressively being recognized as a serious social and criminal problem.

Love obsession stalkers represent 20 to 25% of all stalking cases. Love obsession stalkers develop an obsession or fixation on a person with whom they have no personal relationship. Characteristics include developing a fixation on celebrities, co-workers, aerobics instructors, casual acquaintances or people they pass on the street. They display common emotions and motivations such as anger, hostility, obsession, rage at abandonment, loneliness, dependency, jealousy, betrayal, sexual preoccupation, retaliation, need for power and control, sexual intent, attempted reconciliation, projection of blame, humiliation and shame, social incompetence, envy, recent loss, distress over divorce, under the influence of alcohol/drugs, distress over custody dispute and grief.

They are unable to develop relationships through socially acceptable means and attempt to live out their fantasies through their victims. They expect their victims to the play roles as well. The stalkers use threats and intimidation when the victim refuses to respond. Then turn to violence when threats and intimidation fail.

They pursue and intimidate their victims by making a drastic amount of telephone calls, sending letters and unwanted gifts, driving by the victim's home, office, or school, trespassing on property, following the victim, expressing affection, intruding on the victim's family, friends, or coworkers, intruding in private interactions, vandalizing the victim's property, using surveillance techniques, attempting to break and enter into the victim's home, stealing or damaging the victim's possessions, involving the victim in unwanted activities and e-mailing the victim.

Love obsession stalkers usually threaten violence, which they are more likely to carry out the act. They suffer from major mental disorders and personality disorders, especially borderline personality disorder. In addition to being bi-polar, it is my belief that Alexis Mason also suffered from Antisocial Personality Disorder. This disorder begins in childhood or early adolescence and continues into adulthood. It is the result of a combination of biological and environmental factors.

The person may have suffered from a history of childhood physical, sexual or emotional abuse, neglect, deprivation or abandonment. They may have associated with peers who engaged in antisocial behavior or have a parent who is either antisocial or alcoholic. A person who suffers from Antisocial Personality Disorder shows a definite pattern of disregarding and violating the rights of others. They suffer from emotional poverty and have a limited range or depth of feelings.

These individuals have a lack of conforming to laws, show deceitfulness in relationships with others, such as pathological lying, using false names, or conning others for pleasure or profit. They greatly inflate their idea of one's abilities and self-esteem, arrogance and a sense of superiority.

They are cunning and manipulative and use deceit to cheat others for personal gain. They are impulsive and fail to think or plan ahead. They have a tendency to become irritable, angry and aggressive and display this behavior by repeatedly assaulting others or getting into frequent physical fights. They have a disregard for personal safety of others and fail to accept responsibility for their actions. They show irresponsibility by repeated failure to fulfill or honor commitments and obligations. They do not have a good work habit and find it difficult to keep financial responsibilities. They have a lack of feeling guilty about wrong doing, and have no feelings or concern for losses, pain and suffering of others.

They display chronically unstable, antisocial and socially deviant lifestyle. They have a need for stimulation to boredom that requires them to have an excessive need for new, exciting stimulation and risk-taking ventures. Their parasitic lifestyle causes them to have an exploitative financial dependence on others. Their poor behavioral control causes them to have frequent verbal abuse and inappropriate expressions of anger.

They are always looking for love, so their promiscuity causes them to have numerous brief, superficial sexual affairs and a lack of commitment to a long-term relationship. They tend to have displayed some type of juvenile delinquency or criminal behavioral problems between the ages of 13-18, which started before the age of 13.

Furthermore, this person has a diversity of criminal offenses, whether or not the individual has been arrested or convicted. They usually know the law and criminal system well enough to avoid getting caught. To the outside world, people with Antisocial Personality Disorder tend to act witty and charming. They are good at flattery and manipulating other people's emotions by using smooth-talking, engaging and superficial charm.

If you find yourself the victim of a stalker with Antisocial Personality Disorder, please protect yourself and your family by following these suggestions.

1. Always pay attention to your surroundings. Stalkers know things about you like your work schedule, driving routes, and daily routines.

2. Refrain from posting vital information on social media websites.

3. Know your state laws on stalking. Put a restraining order on the stalker immediately. A restraining order (order of protection) is a form of legal injunction that requires a party to refrain from doing, certain acts. A party that refuses to comply with an order faces criminal or civil penalties and may have to pay damages or accept sanctions. Breaches of restraining orders can be considered serious criminal offenses that merit arrest and possible prison sentences. Many states also have specific restraining order laws for stalking.

4. Document every incident as thoroughly as possible, including collecting/keeping videotapes, audiotapes, phone answering machine messages, photos of property damage, letters received, objects left, affidavits from eyewitnesses, and notes. Keep a

journal to document all incidents, including the time, date, and other relevant information for each.

5. Get an alarm system with a motion detector or a video camera on your home.

6. Protect yourself by getting a legal gun in your home. Do not carry a gun, unless you have a legal permit that allows you to do so. Check your state laws.

7. Make sure your family and friends are aware of whom your stalker is (if known) and any identifying information about your stalker.

8. Take a self-defense class and be prepared to defend yourself at all times.

9. Do not give vital information to anyone you do not know. Stalkers may involve other people in their schemes to harm you.

10. Do not take the threats of a stalker lightly.

11. File a complaint with law enforcement as soon as the stalker violates the restraining order. Most states authorize law enforcement to make an arrest for violation of such an order.

12. As a stalking victim, you will feel hopeless and want to give up. Do not lose hope. There may be support networks in your community such as hotlines, counseling services, and support groups that can assist you. Find out about the crime victim compensation programs in your state that reimburse victims for certain out-of-pocket expenses, including medical expenses, lost wages, and other financial needs considered reasonable.

Having a stalker is one of the worst ordeals in the world. You may experience an array of physical, emotional and financial consequences. The emotional suffering that accompanies constantly being watchful for the stalker's next act of harassment may consume all of your energy. You have no idea why the person is stalking you or how far they will go before they stop. You never feel safe. You are in a constant battle for peace and you may lack interest in things you once enjoyed.

You are not at fault for the mental illness of another person. You are a victim. Please remember that this too shall pass. Follow the suggestions provided and protect yourself and your family at all times. Keep family and friends close. Pray, meditate and seek spiritual guidance. Do what is necessary to have a peaceful life.

On another note, do not stay in a relationship where there is physical or mental abuse by a spouse or a spouse's former girlfriend or boyfriend. If your significant other, cannot stand up against their ex and stop the situation from escalating then, you need to leave immediately. This is a form of emotional abuse.

Emotional abuse tears down your feelings of self-worth and independence. You may feel that there is no way out of the relationship or without your partner you have nothing. Emotional abuse includes yelling, name-calling, blaming, shaming, isolating, intimidation, and ignoring. When a person makes you completely dependent on them, then threatens to leave you. That is a form of emotional abuse.

Emotional abuse can be just as damaging as physical abuse. The scars of emotional abuse are real and they run deep. They include having low self-esteem (even if the person used to be confident), showing major personality changes (e.g. an outgoing person becomes withdrawn) and being depressed, anxious, or suicidal.

Each situation is different; however, it is up to you to decide how much mess you will deal with. In hindsight, I should have left Marcus after Alexis kicked me, and he was trying to show her the gift I bought them. At that point, I should have known he would not protect me from Alexis. I didn't pay attention to the signs that confirmed Marcus was not the man for me.

My desire to have a relationship was greater than my ability to wait for the right relationship. A half of a man is better than no man, is the worse piece of advice someone could give. I tricked myself into thinking that real love always had some kind of drama. This is a delusional lie.

Real love doesn't hurt. Real love is caring about someone else's happiness unconditionally. However, real love will not be found until you first love God and yourself. Then and only then will you have the power to stop dealing with non-sense and obtain the life of happiness that God has for you.

It Couldn't Be Done by Edgar A. Guest

Somebody said that it couldn't be done, but she with a chuckle replied that maybe it couldn't, but she would be one who wouldn't say so till she'd tried. So she buckled right in with the trace of a grin on her face. If she worried she hid it. She started to sing as she tackled the thing. That couldn't be done, and she did it. Somebody scoffed: Oh, you'll never do that: At least no one has done it; and the first thing we knew she'd begun it. With a lift of her chin and a bit of a grin, without any doubting or quitting. She started to sing as she tackled the thing that couldn't be done, and she did it. There are thousands to tell you it cannot be done. There are thousands to prophesy failure. There are thousands to point out to you, one by one. The dangers that wait to assail you. But just buckle in with a bit of a grin. Just take off your coat and go to it; just start to sing as you tackle the thing. That "cannot be done and you'll do it!

Special Thanks to all my family and friends for their love and support. Without you, I would not have made it. I Love You.

It is done!

Agape,
Lady LaKeacha M. Jett

ACKNOWLEDGMENTS

There are so many wonderful people I would like to acknowledge and give thanks to. First, I want to thank my Lord and Savior, Jesus Christ. If it had not been for him, I would not be here today. My experiences have led me to have my own relationship with God and to know him for myself; and for that I am thankful.

To the best mother in the world, Cynthia Williams, I love you so much. You are not only my mother, but my best friend. Thank you for always being there and praying for me when I couldn't pray for myself. Thank you for never giving up hope and telling me to keep the faith. Thank you for being you.

To my other seven mothers, my aunties, Aunt Gertie Mae, Aunt Azalee, Aunt Isalie, Aunt Jannie Mae, Aunt Shirley Ann, Aunt Mary Ellen and Aunt Renee, thank you all for showing me what real women do. Thank you for your continuous love, support and encouragement. I have never met another family in which all eight sisters talk to each other almost every day. That is true love. I love you all. A special thanks to my aunt, Aunt Izzy who was by my side every step of the way, and my Aunt Bert who was ready for whatever.

To my uncles, Uncle Zeek, Cousin Balley and Uncle Curley. Thank you Uncle Curley for showing me the way around in Atlanta and always being there when I need you. Thank you for being the strong male figure in my children's life that they needed to see. I love you all.

To all my cousins, you guys are my extended sisters and brothers. I know I will be in trouble for not naming everyone, but I have to say a special thanks to my cousin Lamont. Lamont, you have been my role model since I was five. You have overcome so many things, yet you continue to laugh and create happiness for everyone around you. Thank you for attending all those court dates with me and being there every step of the way.

To my cousin LaShawn, your faith and encouragement kept me going. Thank you for believing in me. To my cousins, Dwayne, Andre, Mike, Shawn, Darrell, Tiffany and friends Nolan, Chris and Troy. Thank you for having my back every step of the way. I know that the situation could have been handled differently, but I'm glad that you allowed me, to let God handle it. I love you all for that.

To my little sister Angie, we have been through so much together and I pray that God gives you all the happiness that you can handle. Thank you for being my rock. Believe it or not, I look up to you because you dare to be yourself no matter what and I love you more than you know. To my nephews, Darrius and Mekhi, auntie loves you.

To my father, James Hammett, stepmother Cynthia Hammett, sister Tiffany, brother Kenyon and sister-in-law, LaKorche and my nieces and nephew. Thank you for coming back into my life and teaching me that it's never too late to reconnect a family. I love you.

To the best friends a girl could have, Tiffany, Chante, Lisa, Karlithia, Kantrina, Thmeaka, Sophie, Zipora, Jackie, Trava and Angela. I know that roads have led our lives on different paths, but no matter what, if I need you, you will be there and that's what's important. You ladies are great examples of strong, successful women, making things happen in your lives, the lives of your children and the community. You are making a real difference in the world and I love you all.

To special angels God placed into my life to keep me on the right path, Erika and Chris. Thank you both for allowing me to take Social Butterflies to another level. Thank you for teaching me about love and charity and allowing your lives to be an example to others. I love you.

To Janae, thank you for all your support over the years and for giving me ideas to become better each day.

To Ms. Thomi, thank you for always being supportive and encouraging in every way you can.

To my Godmother, Ms. Ida, thank you for being so strong and keeping me laughing, even when you are not feeling well. Thank you for telling me to keep going no matter what and never to look back. I love you, Ms. Ida.

To Moses, the best guy friend a girl could have, thank you for always helping me out, whenever you can.

To Kathy, thank you for being my book buddy and listening to all the changes I had to undergo in the process of writing this book. Thank you for being a cheerleader and supporting me through this process. Most of all thank you for not quitting on me, when I needed last minute touch ups.

To Ms. Sharon, thank you, thank you and thank you! You were the one who kept pushing me to finish this book. I can't thank you enough. You saw something in me a long time ago and you stood by me until it was complete.

To Paul, thank you for teaching me how to be strong again. Thank you for listening, but allowing me to find my way back to who I am.

To Bishop James and Pastor Greta Tilghman, thank you for always praying for me and being an inspiration to my life and to the lives of so many others.

To Pastor Michelle Underwood, thank you for being such a great role model.

To all my colleagues and friends in the educational system, if you never hear it again, you are appreciated! You give so much of yourselves to help students become successful and many times, you are unrecognized in your efforts. I want you all to know that God recognizes all the good that you do for your students. You are impacting lives in a very special way and you are making a difference in the lives of the children you teach. Keep your heads up and do what God has placed you here to do.

A special thank you to those educators who served as my mentors to help me to become the teacher and writer that I am today, Elizabeth Craig, James Smith, Lois Stokes, Dorian Brice, Carolyn Foster, Sharon Lee and Shirley Choice.

To everyone who has made this vision a reality; my publicist, GlenNeta Griffin, editor, Melinda Jones and business manager, Lonnie Smith. Thank you all for looking out for my best interest and always encouraging me to keep going.

To my graphic designers, G.B. Designs, C.K. Worldwide, Lynette Jackson Photography and Chantay Davenport, thank you all for the beautiful graphics in my products and websites. To my stylist, Tova Askew, thank you for keeping me up to date with the latest gear and styles.

To my three wonderful children, Dionte', Kaylah and Kai, thank you for loving mommy unconditionally. Thank you for understanding. All of the nights that I was out late, all of the weekends I was in class, all of the meetings, trainings, workshops and events I had to attend, thank you for never getting mad. Thank you for not complaining when things were not perfect in our lives and when we didn't have all the luxuries that we wanted. Thank you for all the hugs, kisses and love even when I wasn't the perfect mommy. You are the best children a mother could ask for and I love you with all my heart.

Last but certainly not least, to the wonderful people who have gone to heaven, but touched my life in a special way, my grandfather, Elliott Jones, my grandmothers, Mary Lemon Jones and Queen "Cissy" Hammett. I love you all. To my sister, Tinika Patrice Jones, you are still my inspiration. To Pastor Julia Williams and Pastor O'Celia Blue (Aunt Celie) thank you both for praying for me. To my Uncle Pook, thank you for being a "real" man that I had to look up to. To my Auntie Dorothy, thank you for loving me. To my friend, Kim, thank you for teaching me how to be happy, no matter what the circumstances are. To the little girl, I would never know, Kellis Alliyah, I love you.

Discussion Questions

1. Do you think Keacha should have stopped talking to Marcus when she found out Alexis was pregnant by him? Why or why not?

2. What would have been the best solution for Marcus once he discovered that both ladies were pregnant?

3. At what point do you think Alexis started planning her attack on Keacha?

4. Comparing Marcus' incident report of the bat and kicking incident to Keacha's incident report, do you think Marcus purposely left out important details? How do you feel about him referring to Keacha as "my friend"?

5. What clues did Alexis give to hint that she was the November 16 culprit?

6. Could the November 16 incident have been a random act of violence? Why or why not? Could the other incidents, unknown telephone calls, mail stealing and the stalking by the white van also be random incidents of violence? If not Alexis, who else could have committed these acts?

7. Why do you think the detectives felt that this crime was a "typical baby mama drama" and did not pursue the assailants as they could have?

8. Is there anything Keacha or Marcus could have done to prevent the incidents from escalating to violence?

9. How do you feel about Keacha begging her family not to retaliate? Would you have retaliated

or allowed your family and friends to handle the situation? Why or why not?

10. Did any of Marcus' actions make him suspicious? Do you think he was involved in anything that Alexis did? Do you think Marcus felt guilty about what was happening?

11. At some points did Marcus seem to be protecting Alexis? Do you think that he was afraid of her?

12. How do you think Alexis convinced so many people to join her cause in hurting Keacha? Would you help a friend commit acts of violence against someone? Why or why not?

13. How would you have stopped Alexis from committing the egregious acts that she is accused of? Were there any other acts that would be considered egregious committed by other characters in the story?

14. Why do you think Alexis finally stopped or do you think she may still keep tabs on what Keacha is doing more than 10 years later?

15. Do you think Marcus and Keacha would have gotten married, if her mother had not urged them? Do you think this caused problems in the marriage? Were you surprised when Marcus finally left the marriage? Do you think he should have left or stayed and worked it out?

16. After Marcus left the marriage, do you think Keacha should have gone back to Baltimore with her family? What challenges would she face being

alone in Atlanta without her family and friends while going through a divorce?

17. Do you think Keacha has really forgiven Alexis and Marcus? Could you have forgiven someone who hurt you and attempted to destroy your life?

18. Do you think Alexis' mental illness played a major role in her behavior or do you think she was responsible for her actions?

19. How do you know if a friend or a family member suffers from bi-polar or anti-social disorder? What advice can you give them? Do you think there are more African-American women suffering from this illness than is known?

20. How did both ladies show a lack of self-esteem as it pertained to Marcus? Do you think women show lack of self-esteem when they fight over a man, stay in unhealthy relationships or don't move on once a man has left their lives? What can we do to help ourselves, our friends and sisters to move on when she is in an unhealthy relationship? Is there ever a time when you should "fight" for your man?

21. Do you think that Marcus should have a relationship with Alexis' daughter? Should Marcus introduce Keacha's daughter to her? Do you think the girls could build a relationship as sisters, despite the drama their mothers endured? What problems could occur?

22. What other strategies could Keacha do to turn her life in the right direction? Is there anything

that she suggested that you may try to incorporate into your life?

23. Was the love of Marcus worth all the drama that Keacha and Alexis endured?

24. Do you think Keacha should have called Antoine when all the drama started with Alexis? What do you think will become of Keacha and Antoine's relationship?

25. Has this story made an impact on your life? If so, please share with your group or via my website.

OVERCOME EGREGIOUS ACTS

PERSONAL REFLECTION JOURNAL

LOVE

JOY

PEACE

LONG-SUFFERING

GENTLENESS

GOODNESS

FAITH

MEEKNESS

TEMPERANCE

FORGIVENESS

Who are you?

_____

_____

_____

What type of person are you? List your character traits?

_____

_____

_____

Are you living the life that you are meant to be living?

_____

_____

_____

Why or why not?

_____

_____

_____

What actions do you need to take to live that life?

_____

_____

_____

What is your mission in life? Why are you here on Earth?

_____

_____

_____

What are your gifts and talents?

_____

_____

_____

How can you use those gifts and talents to complete the mission that you have to complete?

_____

_____

_____

What steps do you need to take to accomplish those goals?

_____

_____

_____

What egregious acts do you need to overcome?

_____

_____

_____

Why is it important to overcome egregious acts that have happened to you?

_____

_____

_____

What is forgiveness?

_____

_____

_____

How can forgiveness help you to overcome egregious acts?

_____

_____

_____

Who do you need to forgive and why?

_____

_____

_____

What actions will you take to forgive the people who have wronged you in your life?

_____

_____

_____

What egregious acts have you committed against others?

_____

_____

_____

How can you seek forgiveness for the wrongdoings that you have done?

_____

_____

_____

What habits will you change to accomplish those goals?

_____

_____

_____

What negative thoughts do you have about yourself?

_____

_____

_____

Rewrite those negative thoughts to positive thoughts.

_____

_____

_____

What is your vision of your future?

_____

_____

_____

What books will you read to motivate and inspire you to be better?

_____

_____

_____

Who are your role models? Why?

_____

_____

_____

What negative people do you need to remove from your life to better yourself?

_____

_____

_____

Write a mantra for yourself that you will repeat each day.

_____

_____

_____

Create a vision board for your new life.

ABOUT THE AUTHOR

LaKeacha M. Jett is an educator, writer and publisher. As an award-winning instructor and certified educator of 14 years, LaKeacha has an in depth knowledge of education theory and technique. She holds a bachelor's degree from Coppin State University, a master's degree from The College of Notre Dame in Maryland, and a specialist degree from Argosy University in Atlanta, where she is currently a doctoral candidate. LaKeacha is the co-founder of Social Butterflies Youth Services, Inc., a non-profit organization that builds the self-esteem of girls. Since incorporating in 2007, Social Butterflies, Inc. has reached girls across five states.

LaKeacha has dedicated her life to developing programs and writing curricula, which combat at-risk youth behavior. She has written two educational curricula, *The 28 Days of February* and *Being The Best Me Curriculum*. The 28 Days of February is a resource guide that enlightens students' knowledge of African American History from Africa to America. *Being The Best Me Curriculum* is a character education program that offers a systematic and effective way to develop character and build the self-esteem in youth ages 9 and older. In her latest project, LaKeacha tells the true story of violence, obsession, and survival though her memoir, *Egregious Acts: A Memoir of Victory Over Violence*.

Encouraging, motivating and inspiring girls and women to reach success is LaKeacha's mission. As a former teenage mother and victim of girl-on-girl crime, LaKeacha continues to motivate and inspire girls by conducting enrichment workshops such as, "Too Cute 2 Fight" and "I Can't Go For That: Sex, Drugs & Alcohol." LaKeacha credits her success to her faith in God and her strong family support. A native of Baltimore, Maryland, LaKeacha currently resides in Atlanta, GA with her three beautiful children.

OVERCOME EGREGIOUS ACTS RESOURCES

WEAR IT, READ IT, DO IT!

T-Shirts & Accessories

Music Downloads

Egregious Acts Spoken Word

by Kathy M. Walters

Psalm 91

by Kaylah A. Jett

Unbreakable

by Dionte Shaw

AVAILABLE ONLINE

www.egregiousacts.com

Made in the USA
Charleston, SC
06 September 2012